FRAGMENTS OF IDOLATRY

FRAGMENTS OF IDOLATRY

from 'Crusoe' to Kid Berg

Twelve Character Studies

DAVID FOOT

FAIRFIELD BOOKS

To ANNE, more than a "fragment"

Fairfield Books
17 George's Road, Fairfield Park, Bath BA1 6EY
Tel 01225-335813

First published 2001

ISBN 0 9531196 3 7

Printed and bound in Great Britain by
Bookcraft Ltd, Midsomer Norton, Bath

CONTENTS

ACKNOWLEDGEMENTS

'Crusoe' was the starting point. I had wanted to write about him for years. This rather self-indulgent book gave me the opportunity to talk gratefully to fellow cricket correspondents and friends of his like John Woodcock. Gordon Hutton, whose mother had married Robertson-Glasgow, was generous with his time and memories, and lent me several of "Uncle Raymond's" wartime diaries. Everyone I visited or chatted to - covering all twelve chapters - was equally helpful. I thank them and hope I was able to show why I liked my subjects, well at least eleven of them, so much.

For my opening profile, I also interviewed two relatives, Isla Tuck and Anne Welch; for Carwyn, I was grateful to Cliff Morgan as well as to the *Western Mail* librarian, Tony Woolway, and a former sporting stalwart of that paper, John Billot; for Alan Gibson, there was much honesty and co-operation from two of the sons, Anthony and Adam (Andrew was seriously ill at the time and sadly has since died) and Alan's first wife, Olwen. I gleaned valuable insights, too, from T.C. (Dickie) Dodds, the ex-Essex opener. Because I had such a high regard for all the people I wrote about, I tried hard to step back and resist any temptation to fawn. That would have defeated the purpose of my self-imposed brief.

Step-son Geoffrey Matthews, his wife Ros and their daughter, Emma, told me what Reg Sinfield had meant to them. So, in the case of Maurice Tremlett, did wife Lee and son Tim. Many helped me in various ways; I list them in alphabetical rather than batting order: David Allen, Keith Ball, Mark Foot, David Garmston, Geoffrey Howard, Paul Musson, Humphrey Phelps and Andy Wilson. I apologise to those I have omitted.

A number of the prints come from my own collection. But I thank all who lent pictures, including Tony Stedall, curator of Somerset CCC's excellent museum, the *Western Mail* in Cardiff and relatives of my twelve subjects.

My profile of Horace Hazell first appeared in *The New Ball, Volume 4*, edited by Rob Steen, and I am grateful to the publishers, Sports Books Direct, for permission to reproduce it here.

David Smith, the cricket historian and statistician from Corsham, checked my copy for wayward deliveries with his usual painstaking skills. By research on my part this time, I discovered that he opposed Carwyn James in cricket matches between Carmarthenshire Wanderers and Christ College, Brecon in 1956 and '57; they took each other's wicket.

I'm especially grateful to Stephen Chalke, adult and higher education tutor, cricket writer and now independent publisher, for rashly and bravely volunteering to take on this book. And, oh dear, I nearly forgot: my thanks to my daughter, Julia, a busy mum and assistant producer at the BBC, who has miraculously found the time to put my words on disk, something I'm pathetically incapable of doing.

INTRODUCTION

Let no-one flatter me by suggesting that my portraits, character studies if you like, are essays. William Hazlitt, known to veer at times towards the sporting scene, was an essayist. So were Charles Lamb and Robert Lynd, who first ensnared me within the literary pages of the beloved and lamented *News Chronicle*. Some of J.B. Priestley's best phrases and insights are to be found in his essays. Many of Bernard Shaw's wordy, prescient, self-indulgent prefaces to his plays are in their way brilliant essays.

I have never harboured haughty aspirations in my writing, nurtured as I was in the school of journalism and often obsessed with the oddities of human behaviour. When I write about sport - mostly cricket - my reflections emanate usually from somewhere between the dressing room and the psychiatrist's couch. I like to observe how my subject plays; even more how he thinks, what worries him. It is true that I have been inclined to study complex, unfulfilled and, in some cases, sad people.

This is a different collection. Of my twelve 'idols', one did kill himself. Another tried to. One died, a lonely man, in an Amsterdam hotel. But I have chosen them because, in their varying ways, they have been my heroes. Not all as cricketers, however; not all as practical sportsmen. My miscellany includes a writer and broadcasters, a rugby coach, a football manager and a boxing champion. More than half I came to know well; only one, Alf Dipper, the talented, under-valued Gloucestershire slowcoach, I never met.

My style, I fear, is as discursive as ever. A thread of regard and affection runs through this book - and I hope it shows.

RAYMOND CHARLES ROBERTSON-GLASGOW

1901 - 1965

Amateur cricketer, Oxford University and Somerset.
Distinguished cricket writer.
Dubbed 'Crusoe' by Essex's Charlie McGahey, who famously
told his captain Johnny Douglas: 'I've just been bowled by an old
bugger I thought was dead 2000 years ago - Robinson Crusoe.'

R.C. Robertson-Glasgow has for years been my literary hero and my unattainable model. There was never a more felicitous wordsmith on cricket: sweet of nature, uplifting, funny, poetic, gently sagacious, a profound student of the human condition, scholarly without ever making it appear so, happy in every word ... and ultimately tragic.

It continually heartens me that so many who sustain an eternal affection for the game, with the pretence that its singular subtleties and aesthetic pleasures have not been eroded by brash, materialistic evolution, are in agreement about Robertson-Glasgow's elevated place among the cricket writers.

Measured by the stuffy standards of those who contend that literature, sporting or otherwise, is composed only of long words, classical allusions and grandiloquent metaphors, consciously distanced from the humble craft of journalism, he has been too often critically by-passed. Maybe he was seen by some as devaluing his work by the manner of his writing. He turned out beautiful vignettes in pencil, even on the backs of envelopes. He fashioned 400-word portraits on fellow players, when others needed at least a column and a half or even a complete tome.

It wouldn't be difficult for me to retrieve fleeting, unconnected incidents lurking in my sub-conscious, to explain partially why Crusoe has always been my favourite cricket writer. I suppose I was much influenced, in the way of small boys whose nostrils tingle with the faint, unmistakable sniff of linseed oil, when I discovered that he had played for my native county, Somerset. By the time I went to my first proper match in the late Thirties, under the shadow of the Peters aircraft hangars in Yeovil, he had given up and was wedged behind a trestle table in the little discoloured press tent. Not that he meant anything to me then; I assumed only my weekly paper bothered with cricket matches.

My father had brought me in on the country bus. He, like most of the male spectators, had put on his best Sunday suit, his only one. I was in a neatly ironed open-neck shirt and white ankle socks. We sat on a couple of beer crates. It was Somerset against Lancashire – and we'd all waited impatiently for the rain to stop. I remember Wellard and Andrews, big-muscled and bronzed, going off at the end with arms round each other's shoulders, ready for their first pint of the night.

It must have been fifteen or so years after that, at Glastonbury where I was by then covering Somerset's game for my evening paper in Bristol. I found myself sharing a billowing journalistic haven with half a dozen other reporters; one was Robertson-Glasgow. It was the only time I met him. He had sat silently behind most of us for the whole of the day's play, eventually scribbling his piece for *The Observer*, I believe. In a quiet, courteous voice, he asked if he could borrow my phone to send his match report to London. Only when he began his dictation did I realise who he was. Nothing in my life was more willingly donated.

As I motored home, it troubled me and I found it hard to understand that the pale, withdrawn man who had used my phone was the same as the gregarious double-barrelled charmer whose prose – and conversation – hummed, they said, with so much affability and humour. On that windy day under the Tor, as I now suspect, the burden of living was etched on a face that had intermittently ceased to sparkle. In a few years' time life itself would be too much for him.

We shall return to ponder the waves of melancholia that engulfed and finally killed him. But this is essentially a celebration of a writer of rare gifts, one who was under-praised, I feel, for the very reason that words, similes and sentences came so easily to him; and also because, on his own sheepish admission, he possessed a lazy pen. 'I'm more than half in love with indolence,' he used to say.

Those who were less than generous about his writing called him whimsical, flippant and superficial. The latter in particular was wildly misplaced. It was no way to describe a classicist. His critics, remote as many of them were from the vibrant flow of humanity, could never accept that when it came to cricket any truly serious writer was able to encapsulate the essence of an epic or even surreal deed in half a dozen paragraphs to be read in a Sunday paper over breakfast.

I have already shamelessly confessed that Robertson-Glasgow remains something of an idol. But was he the best? And how do we start to measure, with anything so subjective? There is a surfeit of cricket literature, by famous writers, from the broader, more academic sense, fanciful and verbose, who turned their highly regarded hands to matches in an English meadow. According to my mood, I have dipped happily into the sporting words of the Quaker's son, E V Lucas; then read in rotation, among so many whose writing I liked, Ian Peebles, Alan Ross, Geoffrey Moorhouse, Derek Birley and Peter Roebuck.

It comes back, in my case, to a choice between Sir Neville Cardus and Crusoe – and if we are bandying around high sounding labels like *literature*, then Cardus must, I say with some reluctance, come first. The brilliance and daring – at times excessive – of his imagery defies challenge. So does the sweep of his imagination and the sheer output that dwarfs Robertson-Glasgow's. It's still in my mind perfectly valid to bracket them together, however.

Their styles and backgrounds were of course utterly dissimilar. For Crusoe, the length of a pitch was 22 yards; for Cardus it was all the way from Old Trafford to the opera houses and concert platforms of the world. Cardus could embroider some ornate and beautiful sentences, though I fancy he invariably had half an eye on the effect they would cause in print. There was nothing self-conscious about Robertson-Glasgow. He recoiled from ostentation and his scholarship was obscured. He, too, could write beautifully – but with a brevity that Cardus would never have entertained. His newspaper sub-editors would have liked more words from him. 'Bit short this week, Crusoe. Could you come up with another ... em, hundred words?' For this definitive minimalist, it was not always easy.

One of his envied skills was that he could distil the mood and balance of a match in a few paragraphs. Cardus liked whole columns. The loquacious Mancunian was congenitally discursive, wandering with liberty-taking nostalgia into a dozen by-ways in the course of a match report. Crusoe liked short sentences and was known to drop verbs altogether without any apparent injury to syntax or style. There was no stopping Cardus and his symphonic brasses in full rhythmic flight. A trenchant opinion would then emerge like crashing cymbals. Robertson-Glasgow's word music belonged more to the strings.

No-one back in the *Manchester Guardian* office in Cross Street altered a Cardus comma, or only very occasionally (and discreetly). In truth, not much ever needed to be changed. His lengthy pieces were for the most part exquisitely constructed and his contemporaries knew he was inordinately proud of his reports. He liked to hear the members at Old Trafford discussing them next day. It must be said, too, that after *The Guardian* moved to London, he became increasingly difficult, pernickety and even at times cantankerous; I have that on the word of sub-editors who handled his copy.

Crusoe was altogether more self-effacing. It was almost as if he were fearful of boring the reader. For all his classical learning, he could write with a surprisingly light touch, ready to share an esoteric dressing room joke. It might be argued that some of his vignettes – much of his journalism was too short to be gilded with any description as grand as essay – seemed too trivial. Yet he could still illuminate them with wondrous shafts of phraseology and insights that everyone else had missed.

All his life, either as a player or writer, he steadfastly refused to take cricket too seriously. That shouldn't imply for a moment that he tended to patronise those who played for a living. He loved the majority of county professionals, just like he loved mankind; but he edged away from any cerebral interpretations in his reports and minuscule profiles. The unerring perspicacity was there; the judgments, technical and human, were unwaveringly accurate. As someone who taught English and read the classics all his life, he cherished good writing. However seemingly uncomplicated his sentence construction, he would summon up a lovely, original phrase and find apposite, if kindly, adjectives to convey the fruitless endeavours of a sweating, artisan bowler or a sloppy fielder.

He was inclined to write as he talked; and he was a marvellous conversationalist. He used to tell friends of the interminable, meaningless sermons he sat through at matins during his childhood. Heeding the lessons of such clerical insensitivity, he pledged privately to make sure he held his readers' attention. It was significant that some of his finest work was seen in the short *Cricket Prints* and those inconsequential, sparingly written pieces that appeared to have no more than a peripheral association with sport, published in various newspapers and magazines of quality though small circulations.

Crusoe and Cardus: the two had the highest regard for the game's history and etiquette – as well as its famed practitioners. Crusoe savoured the quirks of honest, jobbing players and lesser mortals who toiled, at times comically, for their counties. He would, for instance, pause to exhume a virtually forgotten occasion when the ageing, overweight CCC ('Box') Case, a Somerset folklore figure between the wars, collapsed in an undignified heap as he tried to get out of the way of a Bill Voce lifter. Case, self-contained bachelor and slowcoach batsman, eventually staggered to his feet and wandered distractedly off, carrying a stump instead of the bat. That was what appealed to Crusoe: comic inelegance, a touch of the music halls (he loved the Crazy Gang and was apt to introduce Nervo and Knox into the narrative almost as readily as Hobbs and Sutcliffe).

Cardus, too, had his favoured cast-list. On a daily basis he put flesh on his Lancashire denizens, whose whims and wonders had delighted him for years. He embellished their on-field or barside reflections, using the phonetic North Country approximation of the kind of earthy speech he knew so well. Wizened old pros didn't know what to make of him. They were often embarrassed by the wisdom, even erudition, he had bestowed on them.

'But you know, Mr Cardus, I didn't say that.'

'No, but you'd have liked to,' would be his instant retort.

He didn't have too much truck with the literal truths. 'Isn't there a profounder truth?' he'd say. In the context of his engaging self-indulgence in his match reports, such a glib question, thrown back to his doting audience, seemed to have a quasi-philosophical edge. It was usually accepted amid mutual chuckles.

Just like Robertson-Glasgow, Cardus was an inveterate talker. Both relished the opportunity to encroach far beyond the cricket boundary. Cardus wanted to extol the latest guest conductor he had seen, or recommend the next Hallé. Crusoe was more chatty, more jokey and, dare we say, less pretentious. Alan Ross, who succeeded him as cricket correspondent of *The Observer* in 1953, conveyed the essence of the man as well as anyone, in the course of his obituary for that paper in the March of 1965:

> The thing you noticed first was his reverberating laugh. He had, when speaking, a disconcerting habit of thrusting his face right up close to yours, never moving his eyes away, and then swaying out of reach like a boxer, or throwing his head back and laughing. It was a laugh that penetrated all corners of a pavilion, a laugh that, pinning its recipients like butterflies to a setting board, had no gainsaying.

An Angus McBean study of Robertson-Glasgow,
as much stylish repertory actor as cricket writer

He was a man of sweetness and charm, of abiding loyalties and infectious enthusiasms ... He was devoid of pomposity and, as a journalist, never succumbed to the temptation of Johnsonian exhortation or portentous moralising ... If he had faults, they were in the direction of levity, a refusal to treat Test matches as warfare or as anything other than civilised fun.

Cardus didn't laugh much. But he had the advantage of working from a broader canvas. He had a first-hand knowledge of more overseas tours. He had the contacts and the entrées that Crusoe lacked. He arguably knew more famous players, not just those Somerset itinerants of negligible talent invited to pick up a bat on the impulsive whim of the county's registrations-flaunting secretary, John Daniell. Conversely, Crusoe had plenty of friends within the game, knew the majority of the 1948 Australian touring party, for instance, and was never – in that cordial manner of his – inhibited about talking with players, whatever their status. We can perhaps assume, however, that Cardus was better versed, by the accident of birth and circumstances, in the vagaries of human nature. Robertson-Glasgow, by comparison, had progressed through the narrower confines of prep and public school, university and cricket club. It was a somewhat blinkered male-orientated world.

Four out of five, asked to weigh the literary merits of one against the other, would plump without hesitations for Cardus. Didn't he revolutionise cricket writing, taking it beyond Victorian and Edwardian cliché and the arid record of a game's chronology? Didn't he give it soul and invest sublime images plucked from some of the great arts of civilisation? Didn't he stand, rightly, as a figure of literature?

I accept all of that without reservation. But for reasons which I can't wholly define I refuse to go with the majority. I simply read Robertson-Glasgow with more enjoyment. So does Derek Birley in *The Willow Wand*, an excellent book of depth and originality. He set out, as he told us on the title page, to explore some cricket myths. And he took a dig at Cardus' "intellectual pretensions", the kind that sometimes got him into a muddle.

In Birley's well argued chapter on Cardus, he reveals his own genuine regard for Robertson-Glasgow. His criticism of Cardus is powerful and I cull, almost at random, several of the author's more trenchant observations:

Cardus deserves special attention, not only because of the reverence accorded his writings but because his use of artistic courtesy titles has distinct social overtones. In cricket he was apt to confuse style with pedigree. Despite all the rhetorical flourishes he gives us the impression that he is merely using cricket as vehicle for his own loftier purposes. His autobiographies suggest that he may even have felt he was slumming, culturally speaking, when he was at Old

Trafford, rather than at Hallé concerts or the theatre. So he needed to elevate cricket by high-brow comparisons with the world of art ... He seems to be more concerned with what the neighbours might think than with the actual music.

I'm not certain how much he liked returning to the press box himself as the tea interval approached, to take out his fountain pen and start his long report (with images of the day's play graphically retained, and musical analogies already in his head). A few cricket writers have never much liked the bonhomie of the 'box'; they don't even approve of being called journalists. I have no time for them; they are earning a living under false pretences. Crusoe warmed to the fellow scribblers within their conclave.

From the days when he left university, he was not really established in a proper kind of job or profession. His earnings were modest and perhaps that accounted for the same long, faded raincoat that he always seemed to be wearing. He wasn't much bothered by appearance in any case, opting for comfort. Journalism went nearest – despite fragmentary teaching – to giving him a living of sorts. It gave him a civilised rationale, too.

When he started writing about cricket, for the Morning Post, some of the scribes were inclined to be too dour and solemn for his liking. 'The press box at Lord's is just like the Silence Room of Carnegie Library in Scotland,' he said. I think I knew what he meant. The first time after the war when I found myself surrounded by Yorkshire's cricket-writing aristocrats, I felt constricted and out of place. They were *en masse* a dull lot. It reminded me of hometown meetings at the Tuesday Rotary Club where, as a junior reporter I sat between my dark grey-suited editor and news editor to sip my brown Windsor and then make notes on a speech of unrelenting boredom. The atmosphere was self-righteous and intimidating.

I was told by those who remembered him that Crusoe always wished everyone a breezy 'Good morning' when he arrived for the day's play. He did his best to break down the oppressive solemnity with a gentle joke or two. He also wrote pieces in a style which brought a splutter or two of disapproval from the more stodgy recesses of the box. 'I tried for naturalism. Flippancy was never far absent because cricketers, especially bowlers, need flippancy to live and to avoid going a little queer. I was doomed therefore to affront those to whom cricket is a quasi-religion.'

The pompous in that box of long ago winced when they heard him dictating. And he used to admit that his editor received letters of apoplectic indignation about "inane asides and abominations", many of the correspondents demanding the return of Sir Pelham Warner with his accompanying sense of propriety. Dear old Plum, for all his renowned prejudices, was an authoritative and prolific chronicler on the game. Yet his prose was often arid, bereft of emotion or a glimmer of mirth. There was

16

nothing gloomy or saturnine about Crusoe's printed words. To read him was to nod the head and laugh out loud.

I'm not sure what he would have made of cricket writing nowadays. The monastic misery has long gone. There's a chirpy, companionable aura in the box. Repartee is sharp. Incestuous jokes are traded, legs are pulled. The glum and the self-important don't last five minutes. We drink and eat and talk cricket lovingly together. He would have liked that, especially the banter. He was a classless man who as a player had as many friends among the professionals as the amateurs. His blue Scottish eyes twinkled as the pros dispensed the latest dressing-room gossip. In the same way he eavesdropped and chuckled aloud at the re-telling of a dozen Fleet Street indiscretions. 'Glasgie's one of us,' they used to say. And he loved that kind of compliment from his Saturday-afternoon peers.

As we amuse ourselves by picturing him in a modern setting, the hilariously unthinkable occurs. Whatever would have been his reaction if his sports editor had been intrepid enough to suggest that on a wet afternoon he might consider learning the basic techniques of a lap-top. His step-son, who remembers him with much endearment and gratitude, says that Crusoe could do little more, in the technical sense, than boil a kettle. As late as the Fifties and Sixties, he could think of no-one so lacking in the practicalities of life.

Much of the copy he handed, during the week, into the offices of *The Observer* was hand-written. His much quoted *Cricket Prints* and so many of the other short pieces were composed in half an hour, often on the train on his way from the Thames Valley into London, an attachée case perched on his lap as a rest. They were usually written with a black biro but the handwriting was unfailingly neat. The articles were delivered just like that, with a professional innocence that recalled a school exercise book, alterations and a few smudges. Significantly, no-one on the newspaper remembered him missing a deadline.

For some of the longer profiles, used unsigned on the leader page, the paragraphs were appropriately typed, after secretarial help had been enlisted in nearby Reading. There was no typewriter in the Robertson-Glasgow home. It still needed an indulgent sports or features desk, with collective faces of benign resignation, as he arrived with his weekly masterpiece of brevity. 'There were times when a lovely piece, say on Arthur Gilligan or Lord Tennyson, would be scribbled on the inside of an envelope. He had nice handwriting but, by God, it was difficult to read sometimes,' one former sub-editor told me. Clearly the sports operation on *The Observer* was renowned in those days for its good-natured tolerance, as well as the quality of its top writers.

Lap-tops would have terrified him. Nor would he have responded enthusiastically to the demands on the modern cricket correspondent – to scan the ground, the surrounds of the dressing room and even the team hotel for extraneous asides to complement the ritual mention of hundreds and hat-tricks. He actually saw it coming and touched on it in 1948 in his autobiographical *46 Not Out*. 'The pendulum has swung full distance. Dullness is feared and avoided. So, unfortunately, is fact. The News Room has invaded sport ... the technique of the game now ranks below the story.'

He told his chums repeatedly that he was indifferent to the politics of the game. The MacLaurin blueprint would, we assume, have bored him. If he were still around today, penning those poetic phrases and - more or less oblivious to the looming deadline – merrily recounting, at the bidding of a friend with a long memory those forays into the beer tent at Weston-super-Mare between wickets when playing for Somerset, his sports editor would have needed someone else at Crusoe's side to dispense the hard news.

That brings us back to the recurrent comparison with Cardus, someone who had an opinion and had no temerity about expressing it. Was Crusoe too much of a non-combatant for the job? Was he cursed to be a schoolboy romantic forever, unrealistically pretending there was nothing wrong with the game? He disproved that with an article he wrote for the 1945 *Wisden* under "Views and Values".

> The cricket reformers should be more honest about their aims. They talk much about improving cricket in the same way that some talk about improving the breed of race horses. But what they are really talking about is money. They speak as financiers, not craftsmen. To them "faster faster" means "richer richer". They believe that one-day cricket would mean more spectators. I believe it would empty the grounds as surely as the rain ... note that these crude plans for so many runs in an hour and so many hours for an innings are concerned entirely with the batsman. Note, too, that they attribute slow scoring to the batsman's ineptitude, never to the bowler's excellence. The "Brighter Cricketers", for their one-day carnivals, cannot allow for an hour in which survival with 20 runs is a far finer performance than five wickets gone for 60. They have literally no time for the artistry of defence. To them a drawn match is a wasted match, no matter what skill, resource, endurance have gone to its achieving.

His was far from an isolated point of view, of course. He was appalled by what was proposed by the visionaries at the time. He made his opinions strongly in defence of the status quo. And, as the game's confused history illustrates, he got some things wrong. At the same time he demonstrated that, when asked, he could rattle a sabre. I'm certain he didn't enjoy it. By choice, his was the delicate pen of the conscientious objector who walks away from tension and battle.

He started with the *News Chronicle* and was employed by the *Morning Post* for seven years and slightly longer by *The Observer*, as cricket and rugby correspondent, and as a regular golf reporter. Later he wrote a weekly column for the *Sunday Times*. He was a gloriously deceptive writer. Behind the witticisms was a layer of wisdom if you cared to look for it. Despite his insistence that he never wanted to take cricket too seriously, one found a core of sanity and good sense. As in the best theatre, of course, comedy and more weighty matters nudge and intertwine.

His obsessive contempt for pomposity was evident in so much of his writing. He didn't go in for words which lost their point when the reader was forced to go in search of the dictionary. A purist in the use of English, he wasn't averse to dispensing with verbs or – maybe in defiance of his schooling – sprinkling sentences of two or three words only into the narrative, to give it almost a "tabloidy" pace. He may have chatted non-stop in the box but he missed little. He possessed a reporter's acute eye for observation. If it was a comical, unavailing effort by a portly fielder on the third-man boundary, so much the better. Once he was mesmerised by the sight of a classical scholar with a therapeutic fondness for cricket, stationed at mid-on and between the fall of wickets, pulling a pipe from his flannels and smoking it. He'd apparently kept it alight in his pocket. In his account of the incident, Crusoe tells us that the fielder smoked through most of the day and had his first pipe of baccy with the morning bath.

Robertson-Glasgow refused to delve for obscure figures of speech, though he was well qualified to dip into Greek mythology. His imagery came without affectation. When he wrote about an Essex-Somerset match at Southend in the Twenties, he playfully told us: 'The pitch, like Jezebel, was fast and unaccountable.' He became lyrical every time he wrote about Denis Compton. 'The song of his bat is as natural as summer's warmth.' Who needed more than that?

There was unforced poetry in much of his work, maybe just below the surface. Some of his verses were published in *The Cricketer*; a few were passing moments of uneasy emotion, intensely personal, as he doodled on a miserable winter's day at home. They were too hastily relegated to the bin or engulfed by the philistine flames of his log fire. Just as much of his newspaper work was ephemeral, so he argued were many of his private, troubled thoughts. Setting them down on non-judgmental fragments of paper was part of the catharsis he needed.

Troubled thoughts, did we say? It is time to consider them. He loved company and fellowship. Almost everything he said or wrote carried an uplifting, usually vivacious message on the human condition. Ivor Brown told us how much Robertson-Glasgow liked life. There couldn't be a more disturbing irony, therefore, than the fact that he died by his own hand at the age of 63.

He was a manic depressive, although like so many who have suffered similarly he tried to keep his illness and its fearful manifestations out of sight. One cousin, who herself knew at first hand those periodic anxieties, recalled how he made certain never to inflict his condition on others. There was whispered talk within the family of "the little black dog", the euphemism for his mental illness.

In his autobiography, he again did his best to avoid the painful and debilitating subject altogether. When his story got to the Christmas term of 1922 (at Corpus Christi College, Oxford), he wrote: 'This chapter is concerned with cricket, not neurology.' But he knew he'd have to make some reference, however cursory, to this low point in his life.

> I was ordered to rest by the doctors. I was sleeping badly and when I began to despise the pleasure of the table, I knew that things were out of joint. No name was given to the ailment which was, in fact, a considerable nervous breakdown ... I will rest content with the remark that only those who have suffered it know the hell of a nervous breakdown. This much of good has come from it all; first, that I have learnt to regard physical ailments with the contempt that nine-tenths of them deserve; and secondly, that I know the unutterable delight of health found after a long and seemingly hopeless search.

That was as near as he ever went to sharing his inner wretchedness with others. His breakdown was the first of a number that dogged him, confining him to domestic isolation or in several cases to lengthy stays in mental hospitals.

There were times when he drank too much, like the mother he idolised and who might in return have offered a more tactile relationship. It's hard to say whether he used alcohol to anaesthetise himself against the mental demons. In the good times, of which there were many, he drank pints of beer in mannish bravado with his fellow undergraduates. So he did a few years later, this time with journalists, when he was introduced to some of the watering holes adjacent to Fleet Street. That kind of civilised social drinking wasn't a problem.

But he also drank a good deal of whisky, described to me as "the generic family tipple". There is evidence that he was close to becoming an alcoholic in the late Twenties and early Thirties. For a man temperate by nature, so amiably in control, we have to ask ourselves how much the lurking, insidious depression was to blame.

Surprisingly few, and that includes a number of his relatives, were aware either of his illness or his drinking. At those times when family children, all of whom he loved dearly, were around, he was inclined to stay out of sight. Excuses were made for him during his prolonged visits to mental hospitals in Northampton and Bournemouth. One relative told me: 'There were also occasions when we saw him and he was on a high, revelling in young people's company around him. But I remember unexplained words to the effect that he wasn't very well and had gone away for a few weeks. Just that.'

After the late 30s, he was virtually an abstainer. At the parties he attended, he restricted himself to a glass or two of sherry; at home he poured the drinks for others and drank orange juice himself. His step-son, Gordon Hutton, a Lloyds underwriter, told me that his mother who had married Crusoe in 1943, hinted at "Uncle Raymond's excessive drinking" well before the war. The marriage was indeed one of the few positive things to emerge from the mental illness. Elizabeth had met him at St Andrew's Hospital, Northampton, where she was a nurse and he was a patient. She had previously worked mainly in psychiatric wings at various hospitals.

The wedding day picture

Elizabeth had been married before in 1932 and then had been widowed. She was a kind, good-looking woman, altruistic by nature, and in the stressful years that followed she was unfailingly protective of Crusoe. For someone who had gone through life surrounded by males – his best, unwavering friend had been a red headed boy, Edward Holroyd Pearce, he met as a newcomer at Charterhouse – it had been a welcoming experience for him to build this treasured friendship with Elizabeth. He embraced her, physically and psychologically, on their earliest meetings. From that point on, their relationship was close and open.

The step-son could never remember them having a row, even if Elizabeth had much to put up with. He relied, almost like a child, on his wife. The attention she gave him left her desperately weary. Her only real respite came when he went into hospital again, for up to three months at a time in the mid Fifties.

Crusoe made the first attempt on his life in the early Thirties. He cut his throat and the scar remained with him. The family visited the hospital to where he'd been taken. His sister-in-law waited outside in the car while the menfolk stoically went to see him. Returning in silence, they simply drove home again. 'We didn't dare ask whether he was alive or dead. Attempted suicide carried a fearful stigma in those days. The incident was hushed up.'

There followed other attempts to kill himself, with overdoses. Isla Tuck, the daughter of his brother, Bobs, believes he took an overdose and then alerted people. 'He didn't really want to be dead, yet couldn't bear what he was going through.'

In the early Spring of 1965, when Robertson-Glasgow and his wife were living at Lime Tree Cottage in the grounds of St Andrew's prep school at Pangbourne, the 'Black Dog' was once more creeping up on Crusoe. At the time he was organising an informal and very popular Literary Society among the boys. It was also true that he was going to fewer cocktail and sherry parties, maybe laughing a little less, not seeing as many cricket matches - and those in the local villages. By now his only writing was for the *Sunday Times*.

On March 4 the snow was falling heavily. Elizabeth went out with a shovel to clear a path to the gate. It was hard work and took some time. When she returned to the house, Crusoe was unconscious. He'd taken a massive overdose. At the inquest, the impression was given that a morbid fear of snow contributed to the cause of death. Mr Hutton, who lived at home then, is convinced this was misleading. 'After all, Uncle Raymond's mother had a brother who was a leading member of the National Skiing Association. He used to go on holiday with him and though he preferred skating to skiing, he wasn't bothered by snow.'

This conflicts with the general, much-repeated version. 'Poor old Crusoe. Couldn't stand the snow, you know. Felt like topping himself whenever he saw the snowflakes.' Some, influenced by the coroner's words, came to accept "the snow theory". Mr Hutton thinks his mother may inadvertently have given the wrong impression when she was called at the inquest. 'I believe Uncle Raymond's only adverse remark about the weather was when he pulled back the bedroom curtains, saw the snow and commented that, oh dear, it was a miserable day. He stayed in bed while my mother went out to clear the path.' We are left to surmise about his state of mind that particular day.

The circumstances aren't really important. The generous sentiments of affection that followed, the messages and the obituaries, then playwright Ben Travers's suitably loving and humorous address at the memorial service in St Bride's six weeks later, offered some kind of consolation for the family.

Mental anxieties and disorders could be clearly detected in the genes of the various families from whom Robertson-Glasgow sprang. Brother Bobs was not entirely free from them. The novelist, Graham Greene, a distant cousin, suffered from depression and that occasion when he picked up a firearm to play Russian roulette with his life is well documented.

Crusoe lacked the stability and love in his upbringing that might have gone some way towards shutting out the demons. Unlike many of his relatives, he possessed a natural tactility – but more than once he had stretched up his child's tender arms in vain. There was a measure of aridity about his parents' marriage. His Scottish father was no doubt, emotionally, a late developer. One day he was shown a photograph of a girl who was the cousin of a fellow officer. 'I'm going to marry her,' he announced to everyone's surprise after taking a long, analytical look. And he did. She'd been brought up in an East Anglian rectory. She was tall, attractive and independent. Crusoe described her as 'very beautiful'. He was devoted to her and saw no flaw at all in a personality that was intelligent, assertive but ultimately wayward.

He had a deep love of his mother, Muriel – psychoanalysts may be inclined to read too readily into this – and deserved more in return from her. He cherished the way she looked, her intellect, the way she read, too rarely, to the young brothers their stories after bedside prayers at night. But yes, too rarely. 'Just to be near her was enough … though the time we spent together had to be counted in days, not borrowed freely from eternity,' he was to write with a reflective sadness.

His parents' marriage wasn't a particularly happy one. The father, Major Robert, often known as Bertie, was a regular soldier for some years. He was the definitive dour Scot, more interested in fishing than domestic responsibilities or making a fuss of a wife who could be too individualistic and was subject to whims and moods. One member of the family went as far as to say: 'I'd describe the marriage as a disaster. Raymond's father married an image rather than a real person. She was very independent-minded. In the early days in Scotland she got invited to a party and was surrounded by very glum hosts and guests, but she'd come with a limited wardrobe and wore a dress that met with disapproval. Her husband's sister had just died and it was apparently felt she should be in mourning.'

She was in fact ostracised by local society so the couple moved to near Edinburgh where the two boys were born. Muriel was constantly restless and there was little money to spare. They were always on the move, renting houses or finding temporary accommodation in small hotels. There was little sign of a fixed home, to give Raymond and brother Bobs the sense of security and continuity they needed. The boys, who wandered off regularly to play in the woods, were conscious of the tension within the family even if they couldn't quite articulate what was happening.

The father, who in attitude never quite left the army, failed to communicate with either his wife or his children. 'What's that, Raymond? You like cricket, you say? You should come fishing with me.' The idea was anathema to the boy. 'Father unfortunately viewed cricket as a transient and juvenile form of exercise. Fishing was his passion. Once he had me for three days practising casting a fly at an old hat in the garden, when I'd have liked to be playing cricket.' Raymond's mother, academically bright, was increasingly frustrated by her sterile marriage, in the social sense, and lack of fulfilment. She had no interest in domestic matters or helping to run an estate. Her maternal duties were at times ignored and the boys were brought up in the main by governesses.

At the prep school, St Edmund's, Hindhead, in Surrey, where the brothers attended, the sister of the headmaster told members of the family that at the end of term, it was never known where the Robertson-Glasgow boys would be going. There were seldom letters or instructions from their mother. 'The family arrangements were terribly disorganised. Sometimes we simply had to keep them at the school during the holidays.'

All the evidence suggests that Muriel – despite Raymond's continued blind affection for her – was almost indifferent to her children. She once went, restless as ever, to stay for a few weeks at one of the spas in Germany. Possibly troubled by a twinge of parental guilt, she asked the current governess to bring them over. But she quickly lost patience at their presence, contended they were making too much noise within the decorous setting, and sent them home two days later.

It was a cold, unsettling and emotionally remote upbringing, devoid of any semblance of stability. A sensitive boy like Raymond was left in confusion. He wondered why he didn't see his parents more often. The close friendship of his equally isolated brother and that of other withdrawn and "disowned" form-mates at the boarding school came the nearest to a feeling of boyish fellowship and fun. Just once or twice they freed themselves from this oppressive emotional cage. They were taken to buy shoes for the new term and out of a sense of sheer boredom, the result no doubt of months of confinement, they started throwing plimsolls in all directions. A young assistant, fired by the unbridled chaos, joined in. As for the middle-aged governess, she'd completely lost her grip. The manager in the shoe shop was summoned and order was restored, with suitable apologies. Even more rebellious, however uncharacteristic, was the cruel joke the Robertson-Glasgow boys played on a German governess who was apt to bully them and instil an unnecessary iron discipline. She was off to get married and had packed her wedding dress. The boys opened her case and poured porridge all over the handsome electric-blue garment. The family confidante told me: 'that was very naughty, of course. But just imagine what an abnormal upbringing they had. They weren't occupied enough. They had no-one to love them.'

Raymond went on to Charterhouse and his brother to Radley. This was where Raymond was made to work hard, to acquire the first really onerous disciplines of education. He was admitted on a scholarship which eased the family finances. Sport was finding its place as he moved towards adulthood; he played in goal for the house matches, he eventually opened the batting and bowling for the 1st XI.

Corpus Christi College, Oxford, which followed, was right for Crusoe. It came second to Balliol in classical learning 'but it bore its books easily and was free from Balliol's curse, the snobbery of the mind,' was how he put it. The first ominous signs of mental torment were soon to emerge and he was having to obscure those days when, in the words of a fellow sufferer, Clemency Holt-Wilson, a cousin, "it felt as if the sun had gone in".

There was much he liked, not least the rounds of golf and cricket at The Parks. On only his second day at Oxford, he took his turn to meet the President, Professor Tommy Case, who surprised him by first offering to play some Beethoven or a few bars of modern jazz on the piano. He was attired in a dressing gown as if pre-empting Noel Coward. Then he proffered port while offering a slightly tongue-in-cheek philosophical aside on strong drink. He encouraged the habit and implied that abstainers were cowards, afraid of life and what the world would think of them. In fact, Robertson-Glasgow was already quaffing pints of ale with enthusiasm. Miles away, the congenitally nomadic Muriel, known within this odd family as Boof, was by now having to cope with her own drink problems. The Professor's jolly words to Crusoe were nearer home than he could ever have imagined.

As an undergraduate, Robertson-Glasgow probably lacked intellectual ambition. On good days he studied hard. He was popular for the right reasons: not for eccentric traits and histrionic flamboyance but because he got on with the duds as well as the dons, because he sustained an envied balance between timely concentrations in the lecture hall and inswing at The Parks.

Not before time, we must pause to consider his cricket. He mocked his prowess and encouraged others to do the same. But his love for the game – especially the people who played – was undying. Throughout his life, many an academic, patrolling Oxford's sylvan boundaries with him, would irritatingly do his best to deflect him from the cricket by unfurling self-conscious snatches of Greek poetry. 'Another time, old cock. Let's talk about Jack Hobbs instead.'

Henry Plumb, the family coachman, chauffeur and odd-job man, had been Robertson-Glasgow's first tutor. They played cricket together with a soft ball in the stable yard. 'Keep you arm up high, young Mr Raymond.' And this he never ceased to do. Through his school years and his Oxford years, we suspect he was more boyishly concerned at keeping that bowler's right arm right up and avidly scanning the scoreboard in the daily papers than moving purposefully towards a decent degree.

He quietly fancied his batting as much as his bowling. He figured in big stands, one of more than 200, in house matches. Later he scored a hundred off the Free Foresters and nearly did the same against Westminster. He mentally prepared himself for Oxford: and that meant, in the first place, a blue as a freshman. He went on to play in four Varsity matches, though not with too much success as a bowler. In fact, he took only two wickets altogether. His contemporaries said he was uncharacteristically nervous.

Indeed he did rather better as a batsman. 'The nearest I've been to heaven on earth was when walking back to the pavilion at Lord's after making 53 in 1923 against Cambridge with a borrowed bat.' In 1920 it must have been almost as sublime a moment when, playing against Surrey, his in-swing deceived Hobbs sufficiently for him to pop a catch to mid-on before scoring. Years later, Robertson-Glasgow was to tell friends: 'I still don't believe it – at best, it was a fluke'. We can assume it embarrassed him.

The statistics of his playing career deserve more than a passing glance, though he was not one to be preoccupied, in conversation or winter-evening contemplation, with them. He played 77 times for Somerset and in all took 464 first class wickets. His best season was 1923 when he took 108 at 17.40. Maybe lurking behind that diffident facade was a hint or two of the thespian after all. At Lord's, for Somerset against Middlesex in 1924, his consistent swing was altogether too penetrative and deceptive for the batsman. His 9-38 earned him headlines not only in the *Somerset County Herald* and Taunton's other weekly, the *County Gazette*.

But why had he, a Scot from Edinburgh, chosen Somerset? He hadn't. John Daniell, who in matters of imaginative and even devious residential qualification and selection had no equal, had. The invitation came when Somerset were playing at The Parks and Robertson-Glasgow was among the wickets. 'Why don't you join us – we could do with another bowler.'

So they could. Somerset, with a turnover of unproven amateurs more suited to the guest-list of a country house drinks party, always needed players, especially young able-bodied bowlers. 'But I'm Scottish, no links at all with the West Country.'

'That's where you are wrong. Been looking into your background. Aren't you a cousin of this Foxcroft chappie, the MP for Bath? Family seat at Hinton Charterhouse? Can't get more Somerset than that, you know.'

Daniell was captain, secretary and president of Somerset: not quite at the same time, though it sometimes seemed as though he was. He'd been a fearless hooker at rugby, leading England half a dozen times. Later he was an England selector and his son, with justifiable filial pride, argued that there was never a more perceptive judge of a rugby player. John Daniell was also a Test selector in the early 20s. Whether on the cricket field or in his secretary's office at Taunton, he didn't just fire off an order; he roared. The pros called him 'the Lion of Judah'. He was astute, crafty and pragmatic. If you were invited to play for Somerset, you snatched up your kit and made sure you arrived at the ground on time.

He wasn't any more generous with his compliments to an amateur than a professional. 'Let's see, Robertson-Glasgow, you swing 'em into the batsman, don't you? I don't rate that kind of bowling very highly. Never have. That kind of stuff suits me when I'm going after the runs.' Not that he appeared noticeably full of them against Oxford's handsome, pale-faced Scot.

In Robertson-Glasgow's subsequent career, lengthy but sporadic, for Somerset, Daniell rarely knew what to make of him. He was rather too chummy with the pros, breaking that irksome tradition at the county of social division. He was apt to walk onto the field in a straw hat. He was apt to walk off it, between the fall of wickets, for a half in the beer tent at festival matches. He was always mislaying his restricted cricketing wardrobe. No-one could remember him ever having more than one pair of boots. When he temporarily lost them, he searched in vain for footwear that fitted from other members of the team. In the end he wore his black leather shoes against Surrey, pleading weakly in mitigation that his domestic chaos was in part attributable to an extended party the night before. Such lapses, which Daniell saw as misplaced undergraduate pranks, drove the captain to distraction.

Daniell pointedly threw the new ball to someone else. 'How do you think you can run up to the stumps in those bloody dancing pumps?'

In his first tentative season for Somerset, Robertson-Glasgow was asked by Daniell and 'Shrimp' Leveson-Gower to make up the numbers for a team of theirs to play a two-day match at Lord's against a Services side. But the young bowler woke up in his hotel on the morning of the match with severe influenza. He did his best to relay an accurate message to Lord's. It wasn't good enough for the impatient Daniell who felt he was being let down by this so-called classics scholar. Daniell stormed up to the hotel reception desk and demanded to know the number of Robertson-Glasgow's bedroom.

Years later, in a light-hearted snippet he wrote for *Men Only*, Crusoe recalled the incident. 'He was shown up and saw two pairs of shoes, one large and male, the other small and feminine, outside the door. Without further reflection he burst in and found an elderly Scot in bed with his wife. It turned out he was a Mr Robertson, of Glasgow. Very awkward indeed ...'

The relationship between the Somerset captain and his oddball in-swinger was never so much strained as surreal. He'd see Crusoe day-dreaming in the field or chatting amiably with spectators when he should have been concentrating on the game. He would reproach him back in the amateurs' changing room. 'And don't start telling me what a good bat you are. You'll either be at number ten or eleven. Bridges and yourself will have to sort it out between you.'

Jim Bridges, who had worked in insurance, run a pub in Weston-super-Mare and played for Somerset as both professional and amateur, reckoned the two of them were worth better than that. Once he was undefeated on 99 when the county were all out. And he had occasionally seen Crusoe open for Somerset, proud of his stands with Tom Young, the senior pro, that talented cricketer and brave man whose lungs had been brutally ravaged by mustard gas in the First World War. That capable county cricketer, and finer golfer, Leonard Crawley, liked to recall a match between Somerset and Essex at Knowle, on the southern side of Bristol. 'To my great surprise, Robertson-Glasgow came in first. He played a great innings of such authority that it was hard to believe he wasn't a regular opener.'

Like Bridges, 'Glasgie', as his friends were inclined to call him, loved the conifers and the homeliness of Weston's Clarence Park. In truth he liked most of the grounds, including those that offered him nothing in terms of movement through the air. Southend was an especial favourite.

'Why? Something in the track there for you?'

'You really want to know? It's the cockles and whelks.'

Cricket was all-important to him. And not important at all. In the evening he went to the nearest music hall, to laugh out loud at broad comedy and forget the five wickets he had taken a few hours earlier. His cousin may have been the pious High Tory member for Bath but Robertson-Glasgow, who knew more about the Greek gods than most county cricketers, relished classless hilarity and fellowship.

Charles Foxcroft, MP, and John Daniell, arch manipulator of regulations, may have been responsible for bringing him to Somerset. Yet it is unthinkable that he could have played for any other county. Its quirkiness, eccentric components and minimal success all appealed to him.

> I grew to love that liberal, unhurried and beautiful county as deeply as any native ... There is an intimacy about Taunton that I've found nowhere else. On one side the cottages crowd against the boundary and it seems to a batsman that a good sixer must land the ball on the blue Quantocks.

I chanced to come across a short piece – they were invariably short, of course – he once wrote about his affection for those early days in Somerset. He referred to Athelney Marshes 'where King Alfred committed his celebrated blunder in domestic science' (he couldn't have been turgid in print even if he'd tried). He went out to the villages with Sammy Woods and Tom Lowry for Sunday services, often guests of a sporting vicar who encouraged bowls and tennis between matins and evensong. 'It was a happy scene – and the mere thought of it restores a sometimes waning belief in human nature.' A stray sentence so full of meaning and torment.

He liked the pastoral calm of Somerset; he liked, almost without exception, the players. He marvelled at the stroke play of Jack MacBryan, Dar Lyon –brother Bev was in the same Oxford side as Crusoe – and Randall Johnson. He put the taciturn Jack White ahead of everyone as a left-arm exponent of flight. He chuckled that slogger Guy Earle didn't even know the way to play back. He chatted, too much, with Len Braund in the slips and saw that wonderful catcher put one down. 'It's a bit like fishing, Raymond. I can afford to let the little ones go.'

On holiday for a few days in Torquay, he looked across the main street and saw Harold Gimblett and Rita outside a dress shop. 'Hey, why don't you two get married?'

'Funny you should say that. We're on our honeymoon.'

The pair, amateur and professional, had much time for each other. They had long talks: not always about the game or the fertile acres of Bicknoller, where Harold's father had assumed he'd grow up to help till the soil. In private moments, on a bench in front of the pros' dingy dressing room, they would drop their heads on their knees and discuss the mental torment they both shared. No-one brought more joy to Taunton by his exquisite stroke-play than Gimblett: no-one engendered more basic happiness around the boundary than Crusoe. Yet in the end, neither could endure life any longer. Their suicides, which I suspect they mutually contemplated, when Robertson-

Glasgow returned to Somerset a cricket correspondent and unfailingly hunted out Gimblett, were similar in method and medical background.

As a bowler, above medium-pace, he wasn't far short of a Test trial. He polished and shined the ball assiduously. He was tall enough to get some bounce. Maybe at times he tried to bowl too fast.

Like the man himself, for unavoidable reasons, he was a bowler of moods. His fragmentary appearances at bad times broke the rhythm. He wasn't robust but the heart was big and never less than willing. In 1923 he played for a whole season and his consistency must surely have earned him some serious consideration when the Test selectors met. He took 39 wickets in a splendid run of four matches and ended the summer with 108 wickets. At Eastbourne his figures were 14-106. When it came to the Weston-super-Mare festival, Leveson-Gower, the chairman of England's selectors, was sitting in the members' enclosure in front of the little pavilion where players avoided the splinters and fought for the wash-basins.

'Glasgie' was aware of the chairman's presence: and accepted that it was his last realistic chance of a Test trial. In the Royal Hotel, where some of the players were staying, he furtively peeped round a pillar to see names being scribbled by "Shrimp" on a sheet of paper. He had actually been less effective than usual, however hard he tried, at Clarence Park. It seems that Leveson-Gower had really gone to the seaside to watch MacBryan who went on to play in the trial and score 80.

Robertson-Glasgow harboured genuine hopes to play for his country. He recoiled from any boastful trait, yet occasionally felt there was no need for false modesty. When he played four times for Oxford against Cambridge, the teams were laden with illustrious names. That quartet of Varsity matches produced no fewer than eight England players. Four of them, Arthur Gilligan, Percy Chapman, Douglas Jardine and Gubby Allen went on to captain their country, as did Tom Lowry (New Zealand). What an embarrassingly pale imitation Oxford and Cambridge offer nowadays.

In his autobiography he pondered the accumulation of talent in the universities when he played. He listed famous names and added, rather untypically, that 'Clem Gibson and Norman Partridge, from Cambridge, and myself, were all at various times, good enough as bowlers to have played for England without being laughed at. Anyhow, I have seen several worse than us getting a few wickets in Anglo-Australian matches.'

It's unlikely that any lack of fulfilment as a county cricketer would have troubled him for long. The meagre ambition that we have talked about saw to that. His selection for the Gentlemen against the Players was some kind of compromise in honours. In any case, Robertson-Glasgow was a happy-go-lucky cricketer, ostensibly happy at least, more at ease when exchanging banter with the regulars in the Stragglers Bar enclosure at Taunton than he would have been in the tense, unsmiling rigours of a Test.

He was still on merit a notable bowler, praised by the Aussies' formidable godfather, Warwick Armstrong, by Jack Hobbs and Douglas Jardine, a victim more than once in schools' cricket. The spectators warmed to him at Taunton because he never behaved like a supercilious amateur – of which there were rather too many in the pre war years – and they wished he'd been able to play more often.

His last first-class game was for the Free Foresters in 1937. It was time to try his hand seriously at writing. He needed to earn some money.

Crusoe, largely because of the erratic lifestyle of his parents, never had much cash to spare. He didn't in truth need too much. His tastes were simple. For a long time he'd been a bachelor, most at ease in the company of men and probably asexual. At various periods he helped out his brother, to whom he remained close, and others, with bits of prep school teaching. He didn't really like the professional disciplines, rigid time-keeping and the marking of books, that teaching involved. Journalism, the easy-going kind without a contract or too many phone calls from the Fourth Estate, was altogether more engaging.

His handwritten reports on Saturday afternoons weren't confined to cricket. *The Observer* sent him to the 1948 Cup Final and he admitted he could easily become addicted, at least once a year, to the emotional aura of Wembley. His unpredictable brief also took in the Grand National, tennis, the Bloodstock Sales and table tennis. He didn't consider it was of paramount importance to know all the rules or nuances.

He couldn't drive a car but in the Twenties used on occasions to ride round the country lanes on a motor-bike. The temptation to brake, usually abruptly, and stop for a chat was not easily resisted. If it was with the local gentry, he'd affect dismay at what he saw as Bernard Shaw's verbose socialist rantings. If it was a conversation over the front garden wall with an academic from some Faculty of English, Crusoe would indict, no doubt with a measure of tongue-in-cheek challenge, the modern verse of Auden. If it was an early-morning natter with the milkman, it would be the recounting of a visual joke he'd seen from the Crazy Gang at the Victoria Palace the previous weekend. The humour of Victor Borge, dry, straight-faced, was also much to his liking. So, it must be said, were Jimmy Edwards, Tony Hancock and Ted Ray. He saw no sin in being what the culture snobs regarded as low-brow. That was why he read Edgar Wallace as well as Lamb and Trollope.

Robertson-Glasgow loved the pastoral quiet of Berkshire. Just as he had once loved the solitude of the Scottish woods. Conversely there were times when he needed people around him. He'd sit at the piano (though he didn't play particularly well) and sing in a pleasant tenor voice snatches from Bless the Bride, as he vamped the choruses for members of his family.

He needed no great persuasion. He knew most of the popular tunes of the day. Or sometimes he'd be asked: 'Tell us about what happened in the Home Guard. Go on, Uncle Ray.' Dutifully, willingly, hilariously, he trotted out the stories that the children had heard a dozen times. It was the social mix within the local platoon that he liked most of all – the keepers and the poachers who temporarily forgot their professional antagonism and mutual wariness as they brewed tea in the improvised hut and waited for Jerry to invade. The nocturnal experience of jovial duty gave him an intimate insight of human relationships at their broadest and warmest. Robertson-Glasgow, with his one stripe and ungainly uniform, wasn't remotely out of place. I again go to the family for recollections. 'Just as in village cricket, which he always enjoyed, he assessed people by their personalities and not their station in life. The Home Guard was a rich seam of humour and he could have written the scripts for a few series of Dad's Army on his own. At the same time, Raymond felt he was doing something useful with his Home Guard duties – and I think it was important to him being accepted in another world.'

His wife, by then 40, brought a completely new dimension to his life when they were married in 1943. Crusoe had doted on his mother, blind to her faults and the insensitivity she once showed to him and Bobs. Now it was Elizabeth who became his constant companion. She was his friend and prop; there were times when he almost stifled her with his innocent demands. At the prep school, she confided that her husband needed to be reassured and mothered, that life could be 'very, very difficult.' For his part, he loved her deeply, though probably not in a too physical way.

Her son, Gordon Hutton, from her previous marriage, offers this affectionate appraisal:

> I was ten when I first met him. He relied implicitly on my mother, especially in the later years of his life. I can't remember them ever having a row, even though she had so much to put up with. He was never temperamental or aggressive and I never heard him complain to anyone about his problems. For much of the time after the early 1950s, he was under medical supervision, from time to time going to hospital.
>
> I'd been living in Scotland with my grandparents, but joining up with my mother and Uncle Raymond, as I called him, totally changed my life. I owe absolutely everything to the fact that they married. He gave me a great deal of support. Certainly without him and his kindly influence, I wouldn't have gone to my public school – or gone on to Oxford, following him into Corpus Christi. When I came down, I went to work at Lloyd's – for the first three years as an insurance broker at £250 a year. Uncle Raymond was not well off and didn't really have any great money sense, although he did try to teach me about compound interest. He was nevertheless generous to me and used to give me a fiver when I left to return to London on a Sunday night. By the time he died, I had switched to the underwriting side of insurance and become a Member of Lloyd's. I think he was very proud of my progress.
>
> He was a most diligent correspondent. He would illustrate his letters to me by drawing cats with long tails, often in the middle of a sentence. There are so many endearing things I remember about him – like his dress sense. He had no qualms about wearing a rather ragged green overcoat and squashed old trilby, because they kept him warm. They did *The Times* crossword together every day. There was so much he liked about village life – following the cricket team long after he had lost interest in watching cricket at higher levels. He would take the dog in the evening up to the local farm where he went to collect the milk. Then he would return, whistling Pedro the Fisherman, a favourite of his. It might be dark outside but we would hear him coming.

The one impression I don't want to give is that he was constantly depressed. Between 1938, say, until 1952-53 there were no problems, no melancholy. He was cheerful, healthy-looking and if anything rather noisy. He did plenty of public speaking – everything from Wombwell Cricket Society to *Wisden* and the Cricket Writers. And always there was laughter. He was a gregarious man.

He went through phases of keeping a diary during the war years. In school exercise books, his personalised, if superficial, record of events demonstrated a considerable degree of patriotism. He lightened gloomier days with cuttings from AP Herbert's verse, vintage "Beachcomber" extracts from the *Daily Express*, and cricket reports. He was much obsessed with the weather – as well as Hitler's evil intentions. There were, too, the amusing personal asides:

24 Nov 1939. Very sleepy on waking. Found while shaving that the tip of my nose had a bright red patch on it, not easily accountable after six months' total abstinence. Must use powder or remain a beacon.

28 Feb 1942. Sunday's issue will be under new management, possibly David Astor's. Never heard of him. Hope he will want a weekly cricket article still.

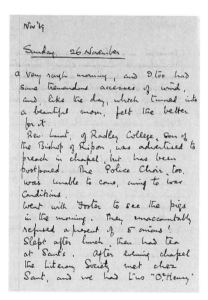

On a rather different level, he observed on 13 Nov, 1942: 'I am bored, like a cat tired of chasing its tail. I believe I would be bored anywhere, except in Tobruk or Tunis just now. They say we ought to get married. Aha! But on what? I see no immediate prospect of an income and if I did, where's the lady? If there was a lady, would she do it? And if we did it, we might become bored.' It's an intriguingly vague domestic commentary, going a full circle and apparently full of apprehension.

Apart from his journalism, he had done a fair amount of broadcasting. The voice was gentle and conversational, the opinions never too dogmatic. During the Oval Test in 1948 he took Gordon with him to Broadcasting House. 'He would do brilliant, reflective pieces, factual but very descriptive, just like his writing. I sat, feeling very honoured, alongside the producer.' Robertson-Glasgow was also a contributor to the Saturday night sports programmes, effortlessly joining in general discussions with personalities like Charles Buchan and John Hislop. His all-round experience as a writer suited the role; and he would willingly talk all night, natural and wise as ever, once the green light was showing. He was briefly tried out as a sports presenter in television. He didn't much enjoy the additional rigmarole and studio disciplines, and preferred the intimacy of radio.

In one early TV stint at The Oval, he told the viewers about the arrival at the ground of the Prime Minister Winston Churchill and Mrs Churchill. A frantic director tried to convince him over his earphones that the occupant of Number Ten at the time was the cricket-loving Clement Attlee. Such examples of amiable absent-mindedness were part of Crusoe's appeal.

But it is his writing, as insightful as it was unpretentious, that we cherish most of all. We can ignore some of the lightweight pieces – though these, too, were invariably lifted by a striking, original simile – and some of those snatches of published work may well have been written under duress or when the demons were gnawing away in his head. Most of his writing was a veritable joy. He counted himself lucky to field in the slips alongside Len Braund and to eavesdrop on the wizened Somerset and England all-rounder's explanation why he had turned down a second benefit: he lost money on the first. We can hear Crusoe chuckling as he writes about it, just as he did when he described Nottinghamshire's C B Harris chatting away to himself at the crease. 'Oh dear, Harris, Harris, what has come over you?' His Boswell listened to and savoured such eccentric monologues.

When it comes to Bradman, there is an absorbing trace of ambiguity.

> At the wicket, he saw what needed to be done sooner than the others, and did it with more precision. He had one eye, as it were, on the heavens and the other on the ledger-book. In the whole game, he was the greatest capitalist of skill. Poetry and murder lived in him together. He would slice the bowling to ribbons, then dance without pity on the corpse.

In that evaluation, we sense the admiration of a fellow cricketer – and a whisper of disapproval.

Robertson-Glasgow was buried in a little church not far from the St Andrew's prep school, founded by Bobs and two colleagues. Crusoe's old cricket-tour chums like Jim Swanton and John Woodcock had been worried for years about his sudden bouts of introspection and the mood swings. Ben Travers, looking himself rather like one of his characters from the Aldwych, said apposite and jolly things at the memorial service; John read a lesson.

Crusoe was, it seems certain, periodically consumed with guilt: guilt over his incorrigible indolence, lack of professional ambition and the absence of a "proper" job; guilt of not being able to do more to wean an increasingly distracted mother off drink; guilt over his daily demands on a middle-aged wife who was too often forced to treat him as an over-dependent child. Nor had he ever been able to cope with pressure, whether it was exams at Oxford or the unavailing search for wickets in the Varsity matches.

He was a fearful worrier. This had been painfully true during the 1950-51 Ashes tour of Australia, where he had been sent by *The Observer*. The rigorous newspaper mechanics and regular filing of copy terrified him. When he made journeys by car, with Woodcock and Swanton, his horror of claustrophobia was evident. 'He always insisted on riding in the front,' John recalls. But the series was far more complicated for him than he had imagined.

Major R G (Beau) Vincent was due to cover the tour for *The Times*. It is true to say he liked a drink. But disenchantment had infinitely more to do with the fact that he was miserable and homesick. He hadn't wanted to go in any case. When he chose to take an early ship from Sydney back to England, *The Times* sports desk was left in a state of confusion. Crusoe was enlisted to help out. He was already assigned to do some work for an evening paper in Australia and now, in addition to his commission for *The Observer*, a generous spirited newspaper which had agreed to pay for his wife's passage as well, he was expected to churn out words and comment for *The Times*. It was the kind of onerous workload that he hadn't previously experienced. And for someone who had naively looked forward to something approaching a relaxing cricket-watching and exploratory holiday, the demanding schedule caused him to retreat into deep caverns of introspection back in his hotel room.

Woodcock, not yet a *Times* writer, had gone on the tour as a freelance. He shared the driving of the hired car with Swanton. Crusoe did his best, as he always did, to hide his oppressive anxieties and with his wife made up a tight, sociable journalistic unit during the many miles from ground to ground. John recalls: 'He was such a sweet-natured man and invariably good company. He and Elizabeth were absolutely devoted. Her role on our travels was to look after picnics.' On top of his incessant deadlines, he had been sounded out about writing a book on the tour. This was no doubt a project that appealed as much to his bank manager, invariably a trifle worried about the family's fiscal arrangements, as himself. The book was eventually written but never published; the uncorrected manuscript remains, suitably cherished, with his stepson. Ironically, *The Times* incorporated much of Robertson-Glasgow's tour copy in a publication brought out by the paper itself. The conflict of interests took him by surprise and he admitted to friends he was disappointed that his own book failed to materialise. Maybe, in the wearying and anti-climactic months on his return, his literary energies and enthusiasms were to wane. After his death, as family and friends attempted to find an explanation for his suicide, his wife said she was convinced he feared the disappearing creative element in his work. There would appear to be some evidence of this in the closing, less fruitful, years of a life in which he had been possessed of such imaginative vibrancy.

The layer of endearing unworldliness didn't leave him. He was a child who went on reading Wodehouse, who would polish off a laden plate of new potatoes as if still a ravenous third-former, who still indulged in harmless lavatorial humour and mischievous bouts of flatulence to the resigned dismay of Elizabeth. A scholar, a poet, a writer: and a child, seldom too sure of the direction.

But emerging from this conflicting amalgam was one of our greatest and saddest cricket writers. There were many generous, loving obituaries, none better than Leonard Crawley's in the *Field*. 'He was much the nicest man I have ever met. He loved life and he loved people. In him there was a deeply Christian trait which insisted that he made the humblest minds of the humblest people intensely happy in his brilliant company.'

In the very first page of his autobiography, *46 Not Out*, a book rich in humanity, though weakened by its uneven texture and what was left out, he wrote: 'To me, everyone is something to wonder at, and I thank heaven for a taste so catholic and vulgar; wonders of knowledge and ignorance, of activity and inertia, of beauty and ugliness. I object to the narrow and mean distribution of what the world calls fame.' Could anything better encapsulate his philosophy?

He could see and enjoy the absurdities of life (and sport) – and write joyously about it. Who else would ever dally so lyrically over a pre-war Somerset batsman who steadfastly refused cucumber with his salad lunch? According to Crusoe, the player claimed that it gave him red spots in front of his eyes. 'And that left him with a tricky decision, back at the crease, not knowing for certain which was the correct ball!' Pure Wodehouse. Or should it be pure Robertson-Glasgow?

Wonderful, cheerful, felicitous, sad, eternally paradoxical Crusoe.

He died with cruel, mystifying suddenness in a nondescript Amsterdam hotel early in 1983, but that coaxing, mellifluous voice can still be affectionately heard, when we listen hard enough, on a hundred Welsh touchlines. Carwyn, just Carwyn: the name continues to bring a glow of treasured reminiscence, followed by those eloquent, perplexed sighs. There was never a greater influence on the way rugby should be played in Wales. Yet, for complex, contrary, needless, self-induced reasons, he was not appointed the national coach. He was the man everyone knew – and no one knew.

Along every valley, in every pit village, every tucked-away rugby ground of steaming winter breaths amid Saturdays' animated throaty ritual, they doted on his wisdom and the melodic words - about sport or life – which he gave so freely to anyone who asked. They basked in his coaching triumphs for Llanelli and the Lions. They travelled miles, many of them miners' sons like himself, to hear him speak. They revered him as a chapel deacon and a white-robed druid. Many contended he was a rugby guru without equal. They were conscious of the lyrical quality that he insisted on bringing to the game, whether first as an instinctive outside half and then as a gentle, single-minded coach, the mentor to so many. What few of them knew was the measure of the pain he suffered in his privacy.

Perhaps it is the voice that we remember best of all. It was musical and sweetly-tuned, too calm, one would have thought, for the biting winds of an exposed touchline. That voice, fashioned by the hymnal, was rarely raised in rebuke at the expense of a player; it increased fractionally in decibels only when someone, in his cups, took a sly, insensitive dig at Carwyn's undeviating political zeal and 'Welshness'. The voice could be mesmeric, full of crochets and quavers and classical allusions, as his unbridled conversation weaved joyfully in and out of literature, the arts and the brotherhood of man. He loved talking, philosophising, paying homage to genius, whether he saw it at the time as Beethoven or Phil Bennett. He had a reasoned opinion about most things. Backed by scholarship and a sharp brain, softened by the chuckle that was seldom too far away, he was not easily shifted from his stance. There were moods of silence and torment, often obscured from his friends and the general public. To them, the voice of Carwyn James was never idle. If not articulating the most practical, cunning or ingenious manner of stifling the All Blacks' pack, it was occupied at tenor-pitch in the chapel pews.

No Welshman, maybe few anywhere, carried out more speaking engagements. On his return from that glorious Antipodean tour of conquest in 1971, when 22 of the Lions' 24 games were won, he was inundated with invitations to rugby club dinners, socials and sports forums. Everyone, even those who had taken an overtly sceptical view of his compounded acclaim, wanted to hear how he had done it, how he had moulded and motivated his Lions to outwit the All Blacks. Some of the invitations involved tortuously long car journeys back to Wales in the middle of the night. Often he was given no more than petrol money, or less. No-one would ever imply he was avaricious. By today's standards he could have had an agent and earned an affluent living from after-dinner speaking alone. But hadn't he once rejected an offer of £20,000 to coach the professional World XV? There was much talk at the time about the looming all-professional exhibition matches. JPR Williams and Gerald Davies had already been sounded out. Carwyn had no qualms about turning down the inducement. With a fierce integrity to reinforce the traditional attitudes then of Rugby Union, he said with old-fashioned sincerity: 'It's strictly an amateur game. I don't want their money.'

The invitations, more often pleas, that came by every post for him to address small and big clubs were hardly ever ignored. If one or two anxious social secretaries waited in vain for a response it was from no lack of courtesy on James' part. His sense of administration was chaotic. He was hardly ever at home, so the letters piled up on the mat. Some remained unopened for weeks; he was a wayward correspondent. Those friends he invited back for a late-night drink discovered the letters, along with his countless ties and books, strewn around the flat.

But he did his best, none too successfully, to be organised. He fulfilled his dinner and speaking engagements as conscientiously as he could. He enjoyed them once he was there. He had learned how to project himself from his days as a teacher and lecturer. He got on his feet and talked as long as they wanted; he wouldn't have known how to be remotely boring. Carwyn spoke without a note, interspersing his appraisal of Welsh rugby and all that it urgently needed to do to improve coaching methods and introduce a more imaginative leadership, with anecdotes plucked at random from his spectrum of experience as a player and coach, at Stradey Park or on the other side of the world.

He could hold a rowdy, beery audience silent and enthralled as he talked seriously, compellingly, about the game they all loved. 'And never once, boyo, did Carwyn tell a joke in bad taste. He left others to trot out the dirty stories.'

In some winter months he was accepting four or five invitations a week. Latterly he was juggling this with his broadcasting and journalism. It was too much for him and he confided to the handful of people really close to him that he frequently felt exhausted. He talked, none too convincingly, of taking a complete break from rugby. "We know how busy you are Mr James, and we are only a little club up the valley. But can you possibly come along and talk to us?" So many requests like that: a commitment too many most weeks. It left him weary and contributed to the bouts of depression that dogged him in his 40s and early 50s. The public never knew.

My acquaintance with him was relatively brief, though I like to think warm. I had been enjoying his evocative, highly personalised Friday pieces in *The Guardian* and at one of our Christmas lunches – I was a freelance cricket writer on the paper – in the *Cheshire Cheese* (sawdust and decent beer) off Fleet Street, I found myself sitting next to him. It was a convivial, decidedly liquid occasion, wondrous for me because he didn't stop talking. Yet, I recall, he was not a selfish conversationalist and encouraged me to tell him about my undistinguished schoolboy career as a prop forward who took the kicks in house matches. That amused him.

The lunch went on deep into the afternoon and I worried about whether the paper's sports pages would ever come out that evening. When John Arlott, then our number one cricket writer, got up to say the few words that were expected of him, I couldn't decide whether he or Carwyn James looked the more flushed. But they were both in wonderful, anecdotal form and I, a country writer romantically seduced by the Dickensian surrounds, was in awe of both of them.

After that I met Carwyn a number of times, either at St Helen's, Swansea, or Sophia Gardens, Cardiff, where I had gone to cover county cricket and he had wandered into the press boxes to join us. He, too, liked his cricket and had done the occasional match for *The Guardian*. It only occurred to me much later that he might have felt I was perhaps intruding on his new journalistic preserves. But from my experience, he was a man generous in spirit and there wasn't the merest suggestion that he would have liked to be writing about Glamorgan those days instead of me.

On one of my visits to Cardiff, long after the close of play, the two of us were drinking together in the small bar above the dressing rooms. Everyone else had left; the players had sunk their solitary pints and gone. I looked anxiously at my watch and told Carwyn it was time for me to motor back to my home in Bristol. 'Not yet ... not yet. Let's have another drink together. We have much to talk about. Tell me about Bristol Rovers. Or Mike Procter. Or John Blake's Bristol – did he really have that lovely rugby team of his running all the time?'

There was almost a kind of desperation in those cascading questions, as he blurted out the disparate potential starting points of conversation. Before I had offered any kind of reply he was at the bar, buying us another double-gin. I was flattered, of course I was, that he wished to stay chatting with me. At the same time, I came to one irreversible conclusion. He was a painfully lonely man.

Cliff Morgan, Trebanog's mighty icon, was among James' friends. They had similar, decent, God-fearing, unpretentious backgrounds. They traded reminiscences by the dozen; they sang hymns together. On that great New Zealand tour, when Carwyn was the coach and Cliff was heavily involved in broadcasting, there was a knock on Morgan's door at half past eleven one evening. 'And there he was, Carwyn, clutching a bottle of gin with the tonic stuck in his breast pocket. Just to see him there made one feel better. He stayed for hours. We had a Welsh song or two, talked about everything – the scoring of tries, the rights of man.'

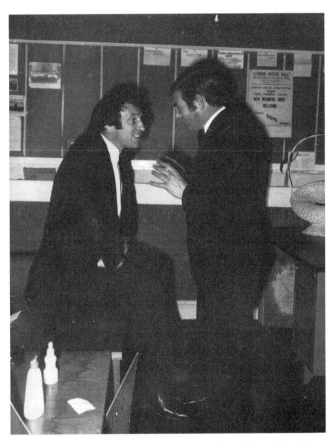

Cliff Morgan and Carwyn, who shared confidential asides, rugby reminiscences and melodious Welsh choruses

Carwyn had played twice for Wales, in 1958, but he was a fly-half destined to be Cliff's understudy. The papers good-heartedly made something of the supposed rivalry, east and west Wales, Cardiff and Llanelli, different cultures, different styles. The two of them joked about it incessantly. James would have loved to play a few more times for Wales but there was not a semblance of envy. There was none in the make-up of the man. 'He only wanted me to do well for Wales,' says Cliff. As a player, Carwyn was described to me as "the silkiest of movers, though giving the impression of wanting to avoid the game's rough and tumble". His suspect defensive qualities may have contributed to his lack of caps.

Once Morgan and James played in the same international. Cliff was at outside half and Carwyn in the centre. 'At one point I asked him if he'd like a spell in my position. He nodded and we switched. But not for long. As far as I remember, the first thing he did was almost drop a goal – and he was close to getting a try under the posts!'

Their friendship remained till the end. Carwyn stayed with Cliff and his wife immediately before going to Holland on that last fateful break. He was due back to accompany Cliff for a match at Twickenham.

'Rugby is a gregarious game and I think, on reflection, it gave him some relief from his loneliness.' Morgan pauses, then recalls: 'Once in a moment of some confidence, he suddenly said to me, "There is a great loneliness upon me, you know." I was struck by his use of words.'

'Oh bugger off, Carwyn. You have so many friends around you.'

And so he had. This is the disturbing dichotomy. Wherever he went, in sporting, academic or political circles, people crowded forward in magnetic attention, either to extol his achievements or just to listen. 'Go on, Carwyn, tell us how you made the Scarlets the best team in Wales, so that they won the Welsh Cup four years in a row ....' Did you really say we should get in our retaliation first? Doesn't sound quite like you, Carwyn ....'

He would patiently say, with Cefneithin eyes sparkling in benign mischief, that the papers got that recurrent quote slightly wrong. One suspects he was less patient with the toadies who asked silly questions and only wanted to tell their mates they'd been chatting with Carwyn James.

Once private barriers were broken down, he liked and needed people's company. He was patently happy among kindred souls: true rugby addicts, the game's thinkers, fellow journalists and broadcasters, *Plaid Cymru* devotees, the intellectuals and the gossips. But when he had shaken the last hand of the evening, gulped down the last G and T, run out of untipped cigarettes and remembered where he had left his raincoat, he was once more confronted with the cruel solitude of a clothes-strewn bachelor flat of aching emptiness.

We must write of his rugby, however. The accepted apogee of his career was beyond question that triumphant Test series of 1971 in New Zealand and Australia. But he didn't need an international arena to convey his innate enthusiasm to others, whether he was playing alongside them or coaching them. He was as zestful when darting through to score a try for his village side, Cefneithin (or to stroke a hundred for neighbouring Tumble), as when he was investing Llanelli with such *élan*. He ignited the imaginations of hundreds of schoolboys, by inviting them to enjoy the game as they played, and never preaching to them. He retrieved the boys who were thinking of defecting to soccer.

John Dawes captained the British Lions on that famous tour. He had similar thoughts, tactically, about how rugby should be played. He had no doubts at all about Carwyn's ability. 'He was the greatest coach the world has ever seen.' Gareth Edwards saw him as someone who got the best out of his players without aggression. Wales had some brilliant contemporaries and they are virtually unanimous in their regard for James' coaching methods and approach.

It's probably true to say that Carwyn saw rugby, for all its physical whims, as a cerebral game. The brawling and blaspheming didn't interest him. He encouraged his teams to play with their heads, to think what they had to do, to reject stereotyped notions and the temptations to opt for caution (and boredom). 'Take a risk or two, make a few mistakes. As long as you are adventurers, I won't mind.'

His team talks were full of persuasive words, more pastoral, poetic and Bardic even than anything the players had heard before. Not an expletive escaped his lips. 'Here, Carwyn, you sound too posh for a coach. But what you say seems to bloody work.' He was all for expanding individual skills, getting away from the predictably orthodox. A practice session was more than a quiet-voiced monologue of instruction. He constantly asked the players what they thought, goading them to respond and exchange ideas. Cliff Morgan said: 'His technical knowledge of the game was so great. He knew the intimacies – the running of the backs, the packing down of the scrums. And what he advocated above all was that every player should have the freedom to express his inherent gifts. He was not for a moment arrogant as a coach.'

So why, for heaven's sake, why? Why did he not coach the Welsh team? It had surely, in every logical sense, to be him in succession to Clive Rowlands.

In many ways, he was very much part of Wales' inner establishment: Welsh-speaking, white-robed, steeped in the cultures of his native heath, erudite. Yet when it came to rugby, at the highest level in his own country, he was critical and despaired of entrenched attitudes. Maybe his popularity and strongly held views worked against him. Some of the game's hierarchy were exceedingly wary of him. He was too much of an individualist, not receptive to a second point of view, they said. They bristled at his implied criticism of WRU policy and had no wish to see him up-tip the apple cart with his strong, singular presence. All right, he wanted to run the whole show – and he knew he could do it better than they could.

It is also reasonable to conclude that one or two were politically suspicious of him with what they perceived as his Welsh-speaking insularity as manifested at the *Plaid Cymru* meetings and hustings, which he addressed with an impassioned eloquence. Wales was saddled with the *Great Divide*, north and south, divided by the mountains, east and west, Welsh-speaking and non-Welsh speaking. Disparate cultures, mutual mistrusts and unease. A group of Carwyn's political intimates, inward-looking and intense, could be seen as tighter than a Lodge meeting. That didn't always go down too well in Cardiff, where the tongue was more likely to be English.

He had a disdainful regard for interfering committee members or those not prepared to share, or at least consider, his more radical ideas about how he believed the game needed to be played in Wales. He was to write: "If I had my time again I would prefer to be a soccer manager than the coach of a rugby club in which half a dozen or more committee men interfere with selection. At international level, five men with exactly the same 'vision' are called annually to present the game." There is the ring of irony in every word.

Certainly in his later years, one could detect hints of disillusionment. Read what he says here:

> We are breeding robots. We have few thinking players at the moment. The Eighties promise little. Perhaps the drudge and the monotony of club training sessions, where everything is done by numbers, has numbed the brain to such an extent that it is incapable of original thought during an actual match. In some clubs, players are even ordered not to think. So no wonder they take the wrong options at critical times … In the first few weeks of the 1982-83 season, I have watched four of the top English clubs and twice as many Welsh. On most occasions I have been bored to tears.

Gentle-voiced he may have been by inclination but he could be waspish at the sluggish lack of compromise by the reactionaries and those he instinctively knew were not on his side. He could harbour a grievance, too. When he came back from New Zealand, many assumed he was an automatic choice for a place on the Welsh Rugby Union Executive. But he was snubbed as a candidate for the vice president's seat. He put on a brave face, though bitterly disappointed. He was a victim of rugby politics, not for the only time by any means.

In 1974 he was asked if he would like to be considered as coach of the national team. It was the ultimate, and rational, honour but he wasted no time in turning it down. He wrote an unequivocal letter to the WRU in which he made it clear he didn't approve of the present system. There was no pussy-footing from James. He asked a number of pointed questions, listed conditions for the post which he knew they would never concede, and asked to be taken off the list of candidates. He'd been previously outvoted in a rather humiliating fashion; now it was his turn to pre-empt any appointment and in the process let the public know he disapproved of the way things were going. He had wanted, if made coach, to be also the chairman of selectors and to carry a certain unchallengeable omnipotence. They were never going to agree to that.

Carwyn at a training session

His conditions for the job may appear to carry an unacceptable level of arrogance and self-importance. But James, a visionary, would not have tolerated procrastinations by those refusing to blow away the cobwebs. No-one could have been more inclined to the spirit of consensus when it came to asking players what they felt about a particular tactic or experimental move. As the national coach, however, he stipulated an uncluttered and free hand. Terms like the *Big Five* irritated him. So did certain senior figures of some standing he always suspected would never have gone along with his daring.

Of course there were flaws in his personality. He could be too tenacious and unyielding in an argument. His critics called him aloof and distant. Some of his silences were misunderstood. 'You'd sooner talk rugby with a couple of dozen schoolkids than with some of the WRU elders.' And he would, too. Not so long before he died, he wrote a series of trenchant articles in the *South Wales Echo* about what he felt was wrong with Welsh rugby. He didn't spare the horses. And he must have been surprised at the reaction in the paper's correspondence column. "Many of the opinions were one-eyed, ill-informed, ill-considered and unsubstantiated," said one reader. James had argued that the game was suffering because the schools were failing in their duties. The educationalists came thundering back. "I know of no teaching contract that includes a duty to culture rugby football, much less about doing it by Carwyn James methods," wrote one.

No, he wasn't universally loved in Wales, it appears. Over a drink he used to talk of an undercurrent of antagonism towards him. He would colour momentarily in anger and violently rub his hands together. For much of his life he suffered acutely from a vicious form of eczema. There were no remedies and he was forced to live with the painful and embarrassing ailment. At times of stress the irritations increased and he scratched his body unknowingly. The first time I met him, I noticed the strange way he rolled up his coat sleeves but kept the shirt buttoned. This, I was told, cooled his arms while still obscuring the inflamed eczema. He had a handsome face and that was almost the only part of the body to escape the ailment's ravages.

Carwyn James died aged 53 from a heart attack in his hotel bedroom in Amsterdam on 10th January 1983. He died alone while having a shave and he banged his head on the bath as he fell. A doctor recorded that he died of natural causes. There was no post mortem – only profound shock back in Wales and some inevitable conjecture. What was a bachelor doing in Amsterdam? Was there a cover-up? Did those recurrent rumours about his sexuality have any substance? Several newspapers in this country received a colourful account of Carwyn's last hours from the Continent. To their eternal credit, they spiked the story.

Carwyn's sexuality is relevant in one respect. There was much back-of-the-hand innuendo during his lifetime. After the apparently strange circumstances of his death, the rumours surfaced again. It upset his family who were at pains to say that he only went to Amsterdam on his break because the travel agent could find nowhere else at short notice. Whether he had homosexual leanings is our business only in that the ambiguities may well have added to his moments of intense depression and paradoxical loneliness. He was to write: "To know a man's fears is to know something of him." There is eloquence in the vagueness of the words.

Clem Thomas, his captain from schoolboy days, who graphically described him as "a bard among bricklayers", was aware of how well Carwyn's older sister, Gwen, mothered him. 'But he had no wife or children to confide in. He was in many ways a man in torment. He was private and lonely and found refuge in his own and his beloved country's passion for the game of rugby.'

In his excellent memoir, simply titled *Carwyn*, a balanced and intimate study, the Welsh author, playwright and personal friend, Alun Richards, perceptively observes at one point: "He had the most feminine of qualities that were unique in a brash, often combative masculine world, and they made him hypersensitive to the feelings of others."

Most of his adult life was in the company of men: as a teacher, player, coach and broadcaster. It is true to say he was most at ease in their company. Engrained in the mode of bachelorhood, he never quite understood the loyalties and domestic commitments of rugby and journalistic chums who needed to say goodnight before going home to their families. He got on well with women, a few of whom liked to fuss over him, making suggestions for his curtains or carpets, though dissuaded from tidying up his littered flat. He was conscious that people were inclined to question his sexuality; it annoyed and embarrassed him, doubtless adding to his complexes. There were occasions he withdrew, inexplicably to the unknowing public, almost to the point of anonymity.

Life had been pleasantly uncomplicated for him in the early years as he grew up in the pit village of Cefneithin, also Barry John's home, not far from Llanelli. His father had worked on a farm when he left school and later, inevitably became a miner. Carwyn had the benefit of a close-knit family. He did well in the local primary school and then Gwendraeth Grammar School. He loved music and drama, and singing at chapel; at the same time he was adept at most sports. There was even an offer of a trial with Cardiff City – something he shared with Wilf Wooller. He was slim then and naturally athletic. He took to rugby and its nuances with almost biblical fervour, certainly not the only Welsh boy to be so entranced. In the summer months, the subtleties and esoteric mental by-ways of cricket also appealed. Carwyn was capable of scoring centuries and bowling decent out-swingers at club and university level. He joined the staff at Llandovery College – the fine coach TP Williams was acknowledged by Carwyn as his mentor - where he taught Welsh, after his years at University College, Aberystwyth and a short time teaching at Queen Elizabeth Grammar School for boys in Carmarthen. He was also to lecture at Trinity College, Carmarthen. He veered to the arts rather than the sciences all his life. Yet he was equally challenged by the angles and the sheer geometry of snooker. He played all games with imagination and intellectual precision, as well as boyish pleasure.

In the tradition of the Welsh-speaker, he was enraptured by language, whether it was Shakespeare's or the sounds and semantics of a relatively obscure Celtic poet. During that happy time when he coached the Italian club Rovigo to success, he voraciously explored local history and the musical, evocative way they spoke. He'd done his National Service, learning Russian at the Joint School for Linguists at Coulsdon, Surrey. I've worked out that we must have been there at the same time, he as a coder in the Royal Navy and I as an Aircraftsman 2nd class. Like me, he would surely have been utterly confused by the range of backgrounds, accents and teaching abilities of those seemingly rounded up to make us, in nine months, into efficient monitors of Russian radio. I didn't last the course. But Coder James, the linguist, would have relished the demanding nightly ritual of learning new, strange-sounding words. Not much time left over for sport then, though on our therapeutic weekend strolls away from the camp we would see the local athlete Gordon Pirie panting his way round the lanes, grunting his greeting as we publicly admired his feats. Carwyn would have known something about the psyche of the long-distance runner.

We can't escape the politics in any study of James. His nationalist zeal was evident from College days. He ended up the president of *Plaid Cymru* at Aberystwyth; in the years that followed his political oratory was unfailing and at times counter-productive. He turned up at demonstrations. Though he disapproved of the physical excesses, for instance, of the Welsh Language Society, he publicly reinforced many of their contentious sentiments. He opposed the official investiture of Prince Charles at Caernarfon and there is some evidence that Special Branch were keeping an eye on his activities. With all his unyielding convictions, irritating as some of them could be, he retained a solid integrity. That was why he rejected an OBE after the eulogies extended to him over the Lions tour.

In 1970 he stood at Llanelli as the *Plaid Cymru* candidate in the General Election. Labour had a big majority and he always knew his chances were slim. But he enjoyed the outlets to propagate his government-for-Wales views, expressed in bi-lingual vigour. Against most of the predictions he polled more than 800 votes, nearly 17 percent and didn't lose his deposit.

He died a sick man. He'd put on weight, was still smoking 50 a day and had a consistent thirst, with or without company. Some of the earlier ebullience had disappeared. He now watched matches, as a broadcaster or journalist, and missed the sweat of the dressing room. Always an expert analyst of what was happening on the field, he increasingly pondered - in the privacy of his flat or in the car – what he saw as his lack of fulfilment. Should he have stuck to academia? Why, for a man so friendly by nature, did he lack friends when he needed them most? Worst of all, he used to confess that he was falling out of love with the game that had been the constant factor of joy in his life, his *raison d'être*.

Carwyn James remains a riddle. There was the personal ecstasy when he was admitted to the Gorsedd of Bards or when, with a rugby ball in his hand, he talked like a vicarious father to a half-circle of captive schoolboys. There were times when he wondered whether he talked too seriously about his native beliefs and aspirations, not acknowledging a second point of view. Here was his least engaging (or some would contend his most treasured) quality as a Welshman.

The memorial service at the Tabernacle chapel in his home village was in Welsh. Many of his country's most famous and revered players packed the pews or stood in the chapel grounds as the service was relayed by loudspeakers. In the congregation, too, were the WRU officials with whom he had waged his lengthy, psychological battle. Everyone seemed agreed, amid the sorrow, on one thing. He should have coached Wales. 'The job was his but he wanted too much ...' 'Trouble with Carwyn, he just wouldn't compromise ...' 'A lovely, lonely, cussed, old bugger ...'

That was what they all whispered as they walked away, heavy in heart. And as we began by saying, we still hear his name most Saturdays on every touchline in Wales as the ball goes out of play and there's time for renewed debate. Carwyn ... Carwyn, you wouldn't have allowed that kick for touch. We'd still like you around to show us how.

ELIAS HENRY (PATSY) HENDREN

1889 - 1962

Professional cricketer, Middlesex and England.
More than a smile and a silly hat.

Patsy Hendren, everyone agreed, was fun. He is remembered for his silly hat and overwhelming good humour. Spectators, who came to watch him, left the ground with a smile on their faces. He played his cricket like an irrepressible fugitive from an Irish show band.

The game has produced few more endearing participants. The many who saved up their pennies to see him play, marvelled at his skills when batting or when scampering around the outfield. They enjoyed even more his repertoire of antics and sweet-natured excesses. He traded repartee with noisy Aussie crowds because he couldn't help himself – and because it was expected of him. He came out, after the lunch interval, to throw oranges and apples instead of a cricket ball.

We in turn are inclined to describe him in that same spirit of excusable excess. Sir Pelham Warner, not always liberal in adulation when it came to the professionals, led the unstinted praise. He wrote that Hendren was one of the best batsmen in the world, adding that 'no nicer professional ever played the game'. It was perhaps true – and one or two cynical old team-mates noticed it – that Patsy could be singularly deferential in the proximity of Plum. Indeed he even admitted that he secretly tried to copy Warner's textbook motions as he played forward.

Hendren was the most popular player of his day. The cult of the personality is not something relatively new to cricket. By exquisite ability, contentious behaviour and evidence of self-publicity, Grace emerged from his Downend orchard to become more famous than Victoria's most illustrious politicians. In their different ways, Ranji and Trumper were cult figures. The handsome Hammond emptied Bristol offices prematurely in late afternoon, during the pre-war years, whenever he was batting. The brooding, complex SF Barnes, greatest of all our bowlers, might also have been the most magnetic of all, if only he had played more county cricket. Hendren played a great deal, with japes and jigs, and the crowds constantly warmed to him because of it.

Maybe we should attempt to bring balance to this delayed and modest evaluation of a posthumous hero. He was a wonderful and fearless hooker, yet a thoroughly misplaced coach in later life, too amiable by nature to instil the necessary measure of discipline and not perceptive enough to see where a young player of only superficial talent was going wrong. He was a wag and a genuine visual comic – and at the same time, to disdainful amateurs in particular and starchy members, an irksome show-off. Significantly, one intelligent contemporary who played the game at high level, a man neither humourless nor in any sense patronising, felt that the persona of Hendren, as relished by the British public, had been largely created by the cartoonist Tom Webster, whose draughtsmanship and mischievous sense of fun captured perfectly Patsy's distinctive, deadpan facial features, along with the incessant buffoonery.

Long ago when the tragic Harold Gimblett invited me to write his biography, his affection for Hendren was unbridled. On his first visit to Lord's, as a young, unworldly Somerset pro, one still struggling to cope with the psychological turmoil that followed his sensational debut in county cricket, he scored a half-century and was then confined to the dressing room with a pulled muscle. He was there on his own, introspective and ill at ease with the grandeur of the game's headquarters, when Hendren suddenly appeared in the doorway. 'And he stayed with me for the whole of the afternoon. He really was the most loveable, and probably the ugliest, man I ever met in cricket.'

It is true that Patsy had the kind of unbeautiful proletarian face that might belong to the occupant of a corner seat in one of those functional stout bars back in his parents' Ireland. This should not imply an alcoholic flush, more the slightly weary features of a peat worker's plainness. An uncomplicated face, not troubled too much by the superfluous demands of intellect, an innocent face. The raucous, boozy inhabitants on The Hill, at Sydney, renowned for and proud of their insensitivity, were always on nodding terms with him as he patrolled the outfield. They saw him endlessly as a comic figure. They had fun at his expense and he mostly took it in good part, though occasionally there was a justifiable edge in his shouted response.

His parents had come across the Irish Sea to build a new home at Turnham Green. The flash of temperament that came with the family's roots was bestowed inevitably on the children. Patsy, real name Elias Henry, was apt to be called 'Murphy', a concession to his geographical background. According to Andy Wilson, the Gloucestershire wicket keeper who had himself started at Lord's in the Thirties, Hendren winced when the team-mates called him Murphy. 'He hated it.' In the comparative privacy of the dressing room, where extrovert traits were forgotten and when the crowds had dispersed, he'd manifest the outfield labours of a sweltering, unrewarded day, with a tetchy outburst. Denis Compton suffered more than once for his unconventional judgments as a self-confident groundstaff boy and cricketing apprentice. Hendren's rebukes were brief, followed invariably by penitence.

Some time after he had given up playing – and had coached at Harrow, in succession to Wilfred Rhodes, then at Sussex with all the sad signs that it was not his natural calling – he'd been appointed Middlesex's scorer. His handwriting was neat, his arithmetic wayward. Fellow scorers used to tell, with benevolent eyes, of instances of faulty mathematics when he did his best to tot up the bowling figures at the close of play. But he liked still being part of the Middlesex entourage, travelling the country just as he used to as a player from 1907 to 1937, and then conveying his limitless enjoyment of the game to successive generations of new players. The pity is that they are too absorbed by self-interest, too impatient to pause with their illustrious elders and acquire additional knowledge. Every county has wise old men who were once distinguished cricketers. They stroll the boundaries and receive no more than token acknowledgement from the young pros who are often oblivious to the measure of achievement and experience that would be willingly imparted. All of us make the same mistake: too late we wish we had asked more from our grandfathers.

In Patsy's last season as the scorer for Middlesex, I met him for the only time. It is a presumptuous claim, as I sat some feet away on the other side of a long table. Middlesex were playing Somerset at Glastonbury and it was the custom for the hosts, Morlands, to entertain the two teams to dinner for one night at the George and Pilgrim, in the centre of the town. This was always a convivial evening, with pints of strong ale and a few appropriate, if informal, words from the two captains. I was there as the representative of my evening paper in Bristol and, as far as I can remember, I contrived to sit as close as possible to this distant hero.

His health was not good and it was known he was planning to retire. Yet was I the only one to see him still as a legendary clown? I half wondered, in my naïveté, whether he continued to make jokes about being hit on the head by Larwood, whether he was as funny as everyone said he used to be. The reality was a disappointment. He was a subdued, slightly shrunken man, more like a detached guest at a small town civic luncheon. He seemed quietly to enjoy himself, said little and retired early to his room. I'd wanted someone on the top table to jump to his feet and say in a loud voice: 'That lovely little man just leaving the room is the great Patsy Hendren. Only Jack Hobbs and Frank Woolley scored more runs, gentlemen. Only Jack scored more hundreds. And no-one made us laugh more. Gentlemen, a round of applause ...'

Instead, the little man, already a victim of ill health, was on his way to bed. He'd last played for Middlesex 23 years earlier: and now he was almost forgotten.

He died in a London hospital two years later, aged 73. His older brother, Denis, who played a few games for Middlesex and then moved on to Durham, died the same year. The bond had been strong. When their parents, two brothers and a sister had died, Denis took on a paternal role. Patsy was to write: 'I owe more than I can say to him. He was the first to catch hold of me and try to make me a cricketer. No lad had a better coach.'

The younger Hendren played his first match for Turnham Green, after words of sibling loyalty from Denis, at the age of twelve. He weighed less than five stone and didn't seem much taller than the stumps. In one of his early matches for the club side, an opponent objected because Hendren was so small and seemed to be turning the contest into a farce. Patsy referred to the incident in a little book of his, taking obvious delight in the fact that he ran the complainant out.

All his playing career, he was an exceptional fielder. He covered acres in the outfield, to save fours or judge difficult high catches. The showman was never too far away. He had the habit of clapping his hands a few times as the ball came down into his strong thick fingers. At least one Middlesex skipper shook his head in disapproval. 'You'll do that one time too many, Pat!' The thing was, no-one could recall his letting a ball slip between his palms. He took 754 catches after all.

He was supremely fit and the sight of those little legs pounding round the boundary was another strand of the humour he evoked. As a senior Middlesex professional, he developed an endearing, if disconcerting, propensity for by-passing his captain. It wasn't an act of disrespect; maybe he simply thought he knew better and that a discreet manoeuvre might be beneficial. He may even have decided he was due for a rest from the exertions of the deep.

Geoffrey Howard, who played a few matches for Middlesex in 1930, told me what happened during a fixture at Northampton. Jack Hearne, Patsy's great friend, was bowling leg spinners and Hendren was fielding at deep square leg. At the end of an over, he came up to Howard and said: 'Perhaps we could change places'. There had been no question of consultation with the Middlesex captain, Nigel Haig.

Hendren went into the slips with minimal explanation while Howard, the young amateur happy to do what he was told, moved into the outfield at square leg. "Very soon, Albert Thomas, who was batting, received a full toss. He hit it hard but not very high in my direction. It was an awkward one to judge and I only saw it at the last second."

Howard, later to be secretary of Lancashire and to manage MCC tours of India and Australia, did well to hold on to the catch. *The Times* next day praised it. Patsy had grinned and said: 'I'd never have caught that one.' He would, of course. The two, the old pro and the young amateur, then on £90 a year as a bank worker – and close to becoming a professional himself after a recommendation from Ronnie Aird – got on well. Howard remembers how proud Hendren had been when showing him the bruises on his thigh, remnants of his encounters with the Australian fast bowlers at Trent Bridge and Lord's in the two opening Tests. He was a brave batsman, who stood up to pace and leaned back to hook, usually square of the wicket, in the best traditions of the little man. He was also unassuming, though inwardly he knew his worth. His parents had little money and he earned modestly as a cricketer. There had been no real career for him outside the game when he finished playing; in the way of others, it had to be coaching and scoring. In the seasons when he played for his country, the occasional cheque from an advertiser came to him. He advocated the benefits of Phosferine, backed by a philosophical copy-writer's purple prose about 'the ability to knock up a big score on the playing fields or in the more serious game of life ...'

Patsy dutifully informed us that he made a point of taking a course of Phosferine at regular intervals throughout the summer – and that he recommended it to all his brother sportsmen. The multi-purpose tonic, it appeared, cured everything from mental exhaustion to maternity weakness, neuralgia to nerve shock and brain fatigue.

He would have taken some ribbing because of that. But the top players were grateful for their various forms of sponsorship. Egos and bank balances were boosted by the sight of their photographs on the backs of buses and, in some cases, the labels of quack products. Phosferine had a nice, authentic ring about it, even if Hendren himself suffered minimal aches and pains.

Professional sportsmen, especially when they had to battle each year for an improved salary, understandably developed a reputation for fundamental astuteness and opportunism. Hendren, when coming up to his 100th century, had every right to hope for an occasional monetary bonus or two. He needed one more hundred as he went off on tour of Australia. The Aussies, especially those at Adelaide where he had done some coaching and got on well with the locals, were aware of his looming record. There was even talk that Adelaide was quietly organising its own little testimonial fund for him. He kept the secret from his Test colleagues – and was desperately disappointed when left out of the side to play there. So no public subscription: but the feat was soon to be achieved instead on the marvellous Melbourne ground.

Almost as soon as England had landed, they were playing against Western Australia at Perth. Hendren struck immediate form and was out for 96. Dare we say that his mind was a trifle distracted by the financial inducements awaiting him in the next match? It is an ignoble notion, mentioned only in fun. Yet to what extent was it a psychosomatic dismissal?

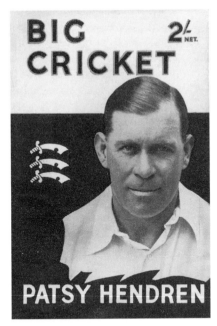

In his book *Big Cricket*, he candidly admitted: 'I nearly made a mess of things ... but I was sent back with my score at 96 and I imagine the bowler responsible must have wondered whether I wasn't a bit mad as, on my way past him to the dressing room, I thanked him quite heartily for having got me out. I can say with truth that was the only occasion in my cricket life when, having got into the nineties, I wasn't at all anxious to reach the hundred mark.'

Elias, or Patsy, or Pat, or Murphy (shush!) was born in 1889 and joined the groundstaff at Lord's in 1905. Like so many talented boys there over the years, he gazed in awe at a succession of great players as they practised at the nets – and he proved himself an unreliable seller of scorecards.

His own progress, which included obligatory stints as a practice bowler, was marked enough to earn him a county debut against Lancashire in 1909. It was a wet and bad-tempered match. Petulant spectators, frustrated by the lack of cricket, charged onto the square. Archie MacLaren bristled with rage and said he had no intention of playing any more in such a highly charged, oafish atmosphere. 'Don't worry, young Pat, it isn't like this every week,' his team-mates told him.

He had to wait until the following season for his next championship match. Not long after, against Gloucestershire, Middlesex won by a single wicket – and Hendren, the unknown little fellow, scored 19 and hit the last crucial runs off Gilbert Jessop who, not very tall himself, charged in faster than anything Hendren had seen before. His older chums clapped him off the field and he wished brother Denis, already gone from the county, had been there to see it.

He didn't immediately establish himself in the Middlesex team. The coaches may not wholly have approved of his stance or some of his less than orthodox strokes. But what a hooker, little feet so quickly into position, and what a powerful cutter. Older lads looked enviously at his forearms; they were thick and hard as iron. Was this the frail 12-year-old who was told in his greenhorn summer months for Turnham Green that what he needed was plenty of plum duff to put some weight on?

The churlish could find things wrong with him. He never ceased completely to be a nervous starter. His innings, whether for county or country, could be excessively wary and uncertain in his early overs. His judgment over a run was notoriously bad. He had fallow sequences that caused him to be dropped from the Test side.

Patsy Hendren leaving the Lord's pavilion with Percy Chapman

Hendren played 51 times for England and scored seven hundreds. His was an uplifting influence on tours, singing as well as clowning, and even getting on his fellow players' nerves. The worst part was always the sea journey; he was a bad sailor and only Jack Hobbs was more wretchedly confined to his cabin. Once the ship had docked, Patsy resumed his effervescence. He was not at times a reliable Test batsman and it was sometimes said he lacked the temperament for cricket at the very top level. Yet the figures hardly confirm that reserved judgment. He had a fine tour to Australia in 1928-29 under Percy Chapman. Then came the 1929-30 visit to the West Indies. He barely left the crease. It was wondrous form.

Four times he scored more than 200 during the tour. There was a wonderful 205 not out against the West Indies at Port of Spain. Those lucky enough to watch continued to talk of his enchanting stand with Leslie Ames. Patsy's overall aggregate was 1765 runs at an average of 135.76. For anyone blessed with imagination, this was an occasion when stark, prosaic figures veered to poetry. The eye, the dancer's feet, the timing rarely if ever let him down. The West Indies were still new to Test cricket – some argued that they had been embraced prematurely – but they drew the rubber, even if it took an aberration of judgment by England's captain, the Hon. Freddie Calthorpe, in the final match at Kingston to allow Karl Nunes' side to survive. No-one ever quite worked out what possessed him to leave the West Indies a total of 836 to win. Blissfully, in a match which was to have been played to a finish, heavy rain put an ironic end to this illogically poised contest. And in anti-climactic mood, England hurriedly packed their bags and sailed for home.

Many of the West Indian spectators might not yet have been versed in the ways and nuances of international cricket – one could arguably say the same of Calthorpe – but without exception they had warmed to Patsy's cheerful and permanent residence at the crease. It was a mutual affection. If he didn't by now cover quite as many acres of the outfield, happy to find himself stationed in the slips for lengthy periods instead, few in the Caribbean could personally make comparisons with the perpetual motion that characterised his previous seasons. He was now 40. And that was still an incomprehensible statistic.

The ageing process was seldom obvious; in fact, some implied that he had never really changed as he was just as wizened in his Twenties as he was when he was twice as old. In 1928, only a year or so before he went off to the West Indies, he had his best season. Nearly every county suffered from his eloquent forearms. He scored 3311 runs, one of three times he passed 3000, and 13 centuries. His runs invariably came at a decent pace. 'I like to get on with it, you know,' he would say in acknowledgement of a compliment.

He didn't mind if the bowler was fast or slow. Just as he enjoyed facing the speed and rhythmic perfections of Ted McDonald, so he grinned as he relished his duels with Clarrie Grimmett, all slow leg-spin, top spin and ceaseless guile. 'Come on, Patsy,' he said in unspoken challenge, 'get after me. Here's one to hit.' It wasn't: and Hendren patted it back with respect. There was more than respect between the two little fellows; there was a friendship which was evident in the hushed exchanges that went on when Grimmett, bald and baiting in the nicest manner, was bowling and Patsy was batting.

'I know how to play you, Clarrie.' And so he did. He could always, better than anyone of his day, spot the googly. When his Test team-mates were in overt torment, Hendren would come to their aid. It was done discreetly, avoiding any suggestion of condescension to a partner. He went for a single off the last ball of the over, not to steal the bowling again but to shield Maurice Leyland, more than once, from the wicked wiles of Grimmett.

His fellow pros at Middlesex accepted that he liked playing up to the crowd. There was no malice in him. He walked away from an argument, hardly ever expressed a strong view and to the approval of committee members was if anything too bland. In print he described Albert Trott's death as 'rather tragic'. It was as if the subject could only be mentioned in hushed tones. But Alberto, a much-liked team-mate of monumental talents and quirks, blew his brains out at the age of 41. He had suffered alcoholism, dropsy, a failed marriage and sexual scandals, and was left with £4 to his name. Just 'rather tragic', Patsy?

Hendren started in an engineering repair shop at five bob a week. He was good natured without academic pretensions, or any real intentions to learn how to be a fitter and turner indefinitely. He was not ham-fisted at cricket. His true friends were Jack Hearne and other pros like Ted Mignon, Joe Murrell and the Aussie Frank Tarrant.

His long summers with Middlesex were dreams of endless joy. He treasured the day he was awarded his county cap after battling against Yorkshire's Rhodes, Haigh and Hirst at their best. The captain, Plum Warner called him into the amateurs' room and made a little speech. Patsy was even asked to go down on one knee. As a good Catholic lad, genuflection came easily to him – though perhaps impishly he wondered, during that self conscious exercise, where Plum came in the Deity.

Just as vividly, in the manner of all county batsmen, he remembered his first hundred, against Sussex in his third full season.

> I had begun to think that I was doomed, always to stop short of those magic three figures … Even that day I was missed in the field when I had made 96. Albert Relf was the bowler who suffered but he smiled a smile which suggested he was rather glad about it … I have made a few hundreds since then but I have only two bats remaining as momentoes, the one with which I made my first century and the other with which I made my 100th hundred.

Hendren failed in his first and last appearance for Middlesex as if getting humanity into perspective. Whatever the visual jokes implied, he could be a worrier. He was upset when Hearne, with whom he'd grown up at Lord's and someone whose style he publicly envied, was dropped by his country. The Test team had been chosen for that particular match at headquarters and Warner avoided eye contact as he passed Hearne after the selectors' meeting. That made Patsy uneasy.

He worried over the inevitable conflict, experienced by every sportsman who played soccer as well as cricket. When he was chosen in 1920 to tour Australia, he agonised for weeks about whether he was being fair to Brentford. There had been times when he and his Middlesex teammate, Jack Durston, who also played at Griffin Park, changed into their football kit during a frantic taxi journey from Lord's. Patsy was a busy little winger, who could accurately curl his corner out of reach of opposing defenders as deftly as he lofted an on-drive which eluded mid-wicket or mid-on. Hendren also played for Queen's Park Rangers, Manchester City and Coventry; his one appearance for England was in an unofficial 'Victory' international against Wales in Cardiff just after the First World War.

Cricket was wisely given precedence when, soon after, he had to decide whether he wanted to go to Australia. In truth, it wasn't a difficult choice. As it happened, a matter of more perplexity was the assembling of his kit and necessities for the tour; in the end he took 16 bats, two dozen shirts and as many ties as he could stuff into his luggage. He worried aloud about what he should take and was jocularly called an old woman. But it was his first tour after all.

He remained in the nicest sense a bit of an old woman. To Tom Webster and the great cricketing public, extending as it did to the vociferous and waspish reaches of the Sydney 'Hill', he was a joker. He worried in private only about little, unimportant things.

The funny hat he once wore was perhaps the biggest and most enduring joke of all. Photographs of his three-peak headgear were beamed round the world. He enjoyed the stir he caused and finally became embarrassed by its recurrence in conversation and picture. He had been given a horrid bang on the head by a Harold Larwood bouncer and was taken unconscious to hospital. He recovered, despite dire fears for his well-being, and before long was to be seen jauntily marching out to the wicket in a protective hat, designed by Minnie, his wife. It was lined with sponge rubber, though more a gimmick than an item of valid armour. Minnie, we can assume, had no intention of patenting the invention.

Maybe, as we were saying, the personality cult has always been an integral part of sport. In Patsy's case, the greasepaint was never too far away. He took a touch of slapstick vaudeville onto the cricket field. And we should have no complaints.

It used to be said that when he walked up to the centre aisle for mass, the congregation would on occasions turn and acknowledge, and smile in anticipation, almost as if he were just going out to bat. I see nothing irreverent in that. Churches don't smile enough.

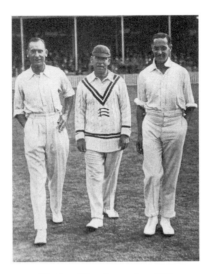

Hobbs, Hendren, Sutcliffe

NORMAN ALAN STEWART GIBSON

1923 - 1997

Distinguished cricket writer and broadcaster.

His voice, with its intuitive phrasing and subtle pauses, his grasp of the varying subjects put before him and, above all, that authority and omniscience, made Alan Gibson one of our finest broadcasters.

We heard him on hundreds of regional programmes, talking about the comic and social vagaries of village life, about poetry, the arts and archaeology, about almost everything, in fact. He introduced "Sunday Half Hour" and constantly amazed us with the erudition he brought to radio institutions like "Round Britain Quiz". But many of us associate him especially with sports broadcasting. He reported regularly on rugby football from cramped stands and less willingly on Cornish touchlines, where he shivered and grumbled, grateful for the Russian-style hat he wore and the improvised Johnson's baby bottle that he pulled from his pocket and occasionally passed to colleagues, equally in need of a warming liquid sustenance of Scottish distillation.

He was best known of all for his cricket, retaining as he did for most of his life a Yorkshireman's love of the game. It was odd that it took 14 years for him to become a member of the BBC's Test match radio commentary panel, in 1962. His contributions were descriptive, distinctive and, in cricketing terms, technically perceptive. Some of his co-broadcasters would admit, in one or two cases a trifle grudgingly, that they much envied his ability with words. Yet in 1975 he was sacked, leaving his many admirers to ask themselves where it had gone wrong. Indeed, where had his whole career and life gone wrong?

Gibson was an incorrigible maverick. It was an integral part of his psyche from which he would never escape. Perhaps he was too clever, too profound, too unfulfilled. A famous broadcaster once told me: 'Alan could be an absolute charmer on a good day – and an utter bastard on a bad one.' That seems to be too facile an explanation. What, for instance, drove him to be such a bastard?

He had many callings and talents. At Oxford he had been president of the Union, gained a First in history without attending a single lecture, and should maybe have stayed within the cerebral confines of academia to take a chair which would surely have been his. He was the son of a Baptist minister and went on to be a Dissenting layman preacher himself, extemporising with all the fire-and-brimstone of old-style Godliness. An occupant of the pulpit needed, as Shaw used to tell us, to be invested with a measure of theatricality as well as sincerity. Alan could perform; during his Oxford days he even found himself taking a leading role in a production of Tourneur's exhumed Jacobean melodrama, *The Revenger's Tragedy*. The curtain went up to discover Gibson, the tyro thespian, holding his sweetheart's skull. He was to write in his autobiography, *A Mingled Yarn*: 'Before I got beyond the first word, everyone started laughing. They laughed and laughed and laughed, just at me standing there.' The audience included dons from Queen's, AL Rowse and John Wain.

In an evaluation like this one of Alan Gibson, it would be improper not to declare an interest. During my own infinitely more modest career, he probably gave me more encouragement than anyone. He also gave me a thoroughly bad time.

As an academic, so precise in his use of English, he repeatedly rebuked me – too often and too publicly, it appeared to me – for careless construction. 'You're always in far too much of a hurry, David Foot. Take more time and you'll be a better writer.' He was a cultural snob (but not a social one) and used me as a whipping boy. When in 1982 he contributed a chapter on Gloucestershire to the book, *County Champions*, written by seventeen different correspondents, I asked him a general, if loosely phrased, question about whether varying style in an anthology gave the publication an uneven literary content. He rounded on me, in a crowded bar, and told me I didn't know the meaning of anthology. 'It's a collection of previously published work,' he pontificated.

It was about this time that he caused a scene in the press box at Taunton, during a Benson & Hedges match against Surrey. Because of the large number of journalists present, our names had been marked out in advance. Alan, who in truth never liked the badinage or sitting with his colleagues, had arrived early and placed his brief case in position. Then he disappeared, in search of a few drinks, for much of the day. Several writers had been forced to sit outside the box and now it looked as though there was a place to spare. I squeezed over into Alan's allocated seat. The atmosphere that day was relaxed and cordial.

But in late afternoon we were all conscious of some pronounced huffing and puffing behind us. Alan had returned from his preferred vantage point in the Stragglers Bar. Suddenly he spotted me in his place and went into a noisy, extraordinary diatribe, which reverberated not only round the small press box but to all corners of the ground. 'David Foot, you are a shit!' And that was only the start of a monologue of undeserved invective. The cordiality of the box had been irrevocably shattered – and I had thought I was a friend of his. He stormed out, only to return half an hour later. He came forward, none too steadily – though his footwork was rarely assured, forcing him to wear faded plimsolls – and whispered in my ear: 'Sorry about that, old chap. Come and join me in the Stragglers. I've put up a double for you.' And he had.

I had much for which to thank him. When we both did match reports for the old West Region, he on rugby and I on soccer, he offered gentle advice and encouraged me not to be too bothered by a script. He spent hours in the BBC club bar after the programmes, *Sport in the West* and *Sports Page*, talking helpfully to print journalists who were doing their best to shed stylised newspaper techniques as they made a little pocket money with their Saturday evening broadcasts.

With some irony I'd made my maiden broadcast in the mid-50s because of Alan's non-arrival in the morning for a county match at Glastonbury. Five minutes of commentary were needed at about noon for the national network. Engineers frantically chased out of the Outside Broadcast van and into the press tent, asking me to stand in. It's possible he remembered fondly; years later, after he'd said his wry goodbyes to the BBC and was being asked as a freelance to do three days of commentary for HTV on Gloucestershire's match with Leicestershire in Bristol, he generously asked me to be his partner. 'Let's make it a nice, civilised conversation,' he reassuringly told me.

Despite domestic and alcoholic demands, he was rarely a big earner. So it was with some reserve that I asked if he would send me five essays for a painfully modest booklet, *Game for Anything*, that I was editing and unwisely subsidising. The Bristol novelist, Derek Robinson, and I would write the other pieces. Alan delivered his contributions which included one on Wally Hammond, the "President of the Immortals"; he explained they were Hardy's words at the end of *Tess*. The booklet, priced at 50p, was naively marketed and I paid my fellow writers a derisory £35 each. They accepted with magnanimous grace.

Alan's father had been a miner from County Durham before becoming a Baptist minister. The only son had been sent to a grammar school and then to Taunton School where, because he was the son of a Non-Conformist minister, the fees were reduced. He stayed for six years and ran away at least three times. Nonetheless he grew in maturity and academic stature, progressing on an exhibition to Queen's College, Oxford. It was the war years and the army beckoned. He had the military police knocking on his door when he failed to turn up for a medical. But he had privately argued that an evening with CB Fry was an obvious priority. His truncated career with the army was spent mostly in hospital.

After Oxford there was a relatively brief and unremunerative period as a university lecturer in the west. Then he intrepidly wrote to Frank Gillard, the former war correspondent who was to be the head off the BBC's West Region, offering himself as a broadcaster. Gibson, the novice, began by reading a short story. Before long, he was presenting and producing his own programmes. Wherever he could, he rejected a script. That sharp mind and spontaneous wit made him a success as an early kind of DJ and in the eventful and experimental *Good Morning*, a waggish two-hander of Saturday cultism with Derek Jones. Between the music were the running jokes, puns and incestuous exchanges. Gibson walked out in understandable rage – not exactly an alien gesture by him – when a harmless gag about one fly saying to another "Woe is me, I am undone" resulted in an absurd and pompous missive from the BBC grandees and his suspension for four weeks.

Some would argue that Gibson wrote as well as he broadcast. As a cricket writer for *The Guardian*, *Sunday Telegraph*, *The Sunday Times* and *The Times*, his match reports rapidly found a legion of devotees. They were like nothing else in contemporary sports journalism. His daily dispatches bore no more than a token resemblance to the events, and even hat tricks, on the field. All of this, it must be said, could both mystify and irritate sub editors who needed to consult the Press Association reports to discover who had scored the century. Gibson was more inclined to dwell on his confessed incompetence as a railway traveller. He regularly missed trains and most of his cross-country sorties, in search of a distant cricket ground, seemed to end up at Didcot station, on whose bleak platforms he was habitually stranded in the small hours.

All his adventures appeared to be underpinned by an absorbing fecundity and air of surrealism. He introduced his doting readership to an unlikely cast-list of acquaintances. They included "GRIP", a cryptic reference to the Glorious Red-headed Imperturbable Pamela, who looked after the drinks in the Hammond Bar at Bristol. His favourite players were seldom high in the national averages. He took to Colin Dredge, the somewhat uncoordinated, beanpole bowler who used to be handed the new ball by Somerset, and dubbed him in print "The Demon of Frome". He was one of the founders and for a long time the president of an arcane little group of Gloucestershire supporters, dedicated to the deeds and unsubstantiated sobriquets that preceded Jack Davey, the one-time left arm fast bowler's surname. The J.J? Society offered limitless scope to those who sympathised that Davey had only one Christian name. The society of 25 members had its own dinner – and own incantations. There were occasions when, at Dover for instance, Gibson moved to a position of prominence on the boundary and bellowed a war-cry of salutations as the startled Jack made his way to the wicket. It was an amiable ritual not far removed from public school and university drollery in Gibson's days there. At times good-hearted, uncomplicated Devonian Davey must have wondered what the hell was happening.

Gibson, the cricket writer, devoted paragraphs to such eccentric issues. He let the *Sunday Times* readers know precisely what he thought of the lack of ice for his whisky available at the Wagon Works ground in Gloucester. He wrote virtually a treatise, back in the late 60s, about the standard of improvised ground-plumbing, appallingly out of keeping as he saw it, with Cheltenham's Regency splendour. The fountain pen which came out in mid-afternoon (when he could find it) was also fearless when it came to his own vices. On the occasion Alan was given a black eye, in the surrounds of the Stragglers Bar, he dutifully reported his humiliation in the next day's paper. Not that he fully went into the reasons for the unedifying encounter.

It should be noted that he mostly viewed play with his back to the field. In one hand was invariably a weighty book of classical substance, in the other a tumbler that was rarely empty. We can avoid it no longer. His thirst was prodigious, dangerously so.

Many of us drove him home or bundled him onto the train. Once at Clarence Park, Weston-super-Mare, long after the close of play, I found him in a state of confusion, trying to work out where he was and why the ordered taxi hadn't turned up. The confusion was at least partially understandable; every entrance and exit at the ground's four corners, looked exactly the same. He slumped into my car and I put him on the train at Locking Road station, not for the only time.

If aspects of his professional life were a disaster of sorts, so was his domestic existence. He was married twice, divorced twice. His first wife, Olwen, whom he met when he was at Oxford, was attractive and influenced by his Liberal zeal and oratory. She lives these days on the Blackdown Hills, just inside Devon and is still a paid-up member of the Lib-Dems. She says she remains grateful for the opportunities, through Alan, of meeting many prominent political figures. With every reason, it would seem, she is less enthusiastic about the kind of marital life she shared with him.

At one point he had hankered after a life at Westminster. As long ago as 1945 he had planned to stand as a Liberal for the Duddleston division of Birmingham, but no-one could raise the necessary deposit. In 1959 he came second at Falmouth/Camborne. Later he was adopted as candidate for Sutton, Plymouth, when Olwen was the local chairman. 'He turned up at one meeting in a dreadful temper and dramatically announced that he was resigning. I responded by quietly saying 'Thank you, Mr Gibson' and, with as much calm as I could muster, said we'd get on with the rest of the meeting. He was always resigning from something or other – and wanting to be persuaded back.'

He was, according to Olwen, a very strong, dominant personality, who could talk anyone into doing anything. 'Sometimes it was persuading friends who had had no previous interest in politics into standing for various elections, as Liberals of course. In my case, it was persuading me to marry him on the grounds that he'd only one lung - which was not true - and would be dead of TB by the time he was thirty. He could be charming when he chose and, as a young man, was very handsome in a wild sort of way - with an unruly mop of black hair and huge brown eyes.'

His drinking started in his university years and could be largely attributed to his upbringing and, especially his mother who was an unswerving teetotaller. 'Alan signed the pledge but soon broke it. He loved pubs, happiest when he had a book in one hand and a pint in the other.' He was a big beer drinker before switching with frightening enthusiasm to whisky. 'Drink only made him belligerent, and he had this frightening temper.'

Alan Gibson who lit up many a conversation with his wit and learning

One joyful product from the marriage for both of them was their two sons, who followed Alan to Queen's. Anthony is the National Farmers' Union regional director in the South West; Andrew is a prominent West Country solicitor. Anthony, who had wanted initially to be a journalist, started instead by writing speeches for the then NFU president, Sir Henry Plumb. He's a natural broadcaster and has been used by the BBC as a freelance cricket reporter.

Alan's own professional life was far too often adversely affected by his need for a drink. I return to his first wife:

> He was very unstable, probably manic depressive, and we never had a normal life, I'm sorry to say. When the family went on holiday to St Ives, he would go into the pub at lunch-time and stay till it closed. Then he'd rejoin us on the beach. On one occasion he said a child threw a stone and hit him on the head. He stormed off and was missing for several days, leaving me alone with the children in the hotel and with very little money. Then he turned up at the St Austell police station, claiming loss of memory because of the blow on the head. We went to rescue him, but no real explanation was ever forthcoming.
>
> As time went on, we rarely had a meal together as a family. He would take his food to the bedroom and sometimes throw it out of the window. Sometimes he would eat it cold for breakfast. Once he put a tin of steak and kidney on to heat and forgot all about it. The tin exploded and the food shot out, to become embedded in the ceiling, tin and all.
>
> He was full of dramatic gestures. Some nights he never came home. We used to lose him quite often. Once he turned up in Manchester and said he couldn't remember how he got there. And this was in the first year of our marriage.

Yet, in the early years, he had meant so much to her. The political and literary conversations rattled away; they had much in common, and much to argue over. 'He used to take the boys on Sunday afternoons for rides into the country. They still think the world of him.' Such stray sentences are full of painful eloquence.

Another isolated reminiscence generates just as many sighs. 'Alan hated to be caught out, you know.'

That brings us to his ghastly nadir, the court case in 1963. He was then forty, an established BBC personality in his own right, still a lay preacher and well known for his religious broadcasts. There was incredulity about the news that he had been fined £30 and banned for a year after admitting that he had driven a car when unfit through drink or drugs.

The prosecution, at Plymouth, told of his arrest at 3am and said that Gibson used "the worst and most offensive language that could be imagined". He had overtaken a police car at 50 mph in a built-up area of the city and weaved about the road. It was about this time that he made his first serious attempt at suicide. In his autobiography, he wrote movingly: "This was all very horrible and must have been perplexing to those who knew me only as a face on the screen or a voice on the air. I am not sure of the causes. My marriage was breaking down. No doubt I overworked and drank too much. For a long time I had been unable to sleep without a very large dose of barbiturate. But when all these and other things have been considered, there was something irrational about it, and this "something", I suppose, is mental illness ..."

As Olwen remembers it:

> After the prosecution for drunken driving, he was in a terrible state because he had been found out. So he took an overdose of barbiturates, having tried in vain to get me to give him back his sleeping tablets, which I'd taken and hidden. I left him in bed when I went off to teach in the morning. When I came back at lunchtime, I found him apparently dead.
>
> He was sectioned, taken to Moorhaven Psychiatric Hospital where he soon recovered, running rings round the psychiatrists and nurses. We visited him there on Christmas Day.

A few days later a journalist friend rang Olwen to say that he and Alan were in the Golden Hind. She didn't know he'd been discharged. She drove to the pub to pick him up; he was happily waving a piece of paper given him at Moorhaven and saying, "I've got proof that I'm the only one officially sane around here!"

Life was often a mental conflict to him, and he sometimes talked of "the Devil within me". It surely accounts for much of his capricious behaviour – heated arguments with gate stewards, dismissive scorn directed at the scores of cricket bores who tried so hard to button-hole him on his way to the beer-tent. Oh dear, how bores dogged him. He was happy to insult them and was wonderful value when he wrote about them. With John Arlott and Henry Blofeld he was a member of the mythical selection committee which chose an English Bores XI. In his book *Growing Up with Cricket*, he was at his sardonic best. He gave bores a fearsome time and, because as a breed they are inclined to be insensitive, they could never quite understand why.

As he shuffled along in his plimsolls, he was rude and frequently offensive, more likely to be in a bad humour in late afternoon. The technical trappings of an Outside Broadcast were beyond him. Left to find a BBC radio box in an isolated cricket ground, needing first to unlock the door from half a dozen keys sent to him through the post, and then switch on the box of tricks left for him, he would become infuriated when met by only an eerie silence – and stomp off for therapeutic sanctity in the nearest pub. He was paid to be a broadcaster not a bloody engineer.

Alan was a libidinous man and fleshy distractions were apt to get in the way. As he approached his fiftieth birthday, he wrote a self-analytical piece in *The Times*. It was printed on the sports pages and he cleverly used cricket analogy to make some of his points. With a measure of frankness, he mentioned that he had played some streaky shots between marriages as he got near his half-century. I remember the veiled reports of his liaison with a younger girl; I knew her and once sat with her on the boundary grass at Bath as she, heavily pregnant, waited for the close of play. His family, I understand, became aware of the relationship.

Gibson began *A Mingled Yarn* by writing: 'I have not been entirely truthful about myself – who can be? Perhaps it illustrates some of the advantages and disadvantages of an upbringing in English religious Dissent. A good book, like a good sermon, often tells you more than its author intends and I hope, or possibly fear, that it may be so with this one."

But he told me that he substantially abridged the manuscript. The scandals, in and out of the BBC, personal as well as professional, seemed to me minimised – and perhaps rightly so. He was not averse, however, to shocking people. For someone so dignified, correct and even pious in some of his outward dealings on good days, the hint of the showman or performer was never too distant. He relished the thrust and theatricality of the hustings. He would come back to the press box, to borrow a phone and dictate his copy in a loud enough voice for lesser mortals alongside him to listen and envy. Once, for a gimmicky cricket match at Ashton Gate, home of Bristol City, Gibson was there at the behest of *The Times* to give his impressions. He arrived late in a bad mood, revealed his utter contempt for the spectacle in sentences that dripped with bile, and clattered out in a curse-filled aura of dudgeon long before the end. The rest of the box had gone silent, bemused by his litany of literary venom.

Never did he shock to a greater extent than when he was asked to review Derek Robinson's acclaimed novel, *Goshawk Squadron* in the early days of BBC Radio Bristol. Alan didn't approve of local radio and resented the manner it had superseded the old, efficient and much cherished regional network. But he knew Robinson, who used to cover rugby in the same Bristol-based broadcasts, and the producer, Bill Salisbury was a friend from earlier days. Yes, he'd do something on the book. It might be critical, mind you …

The programme went out on a Sunday. For his part, Gibson turned up with his script. We can only assume that the experienced Salisbury failed to read it in advance. He was well aware of the reviewer's literary skills and was confident the piece would be impeccably phrased and timed, as ever, to the second.

Nothing wrong with the majority of the phrases or the timing. But Gibson, with what we can only conclude was a conscious use of words in character-assassination, described Robinson's anti-hero as … "a complete cunt".

I listened at home and almost fell off my seat. The producer was left biting his lip. Gibson got up and walked out of the studio as if nothing untoward had happened. It was probably the first time the c-word had ever been used on the BBC: and on a Sunday, too. Spoken by a lay-preacher. The astonishing thing was there were no comebacks, no phone calls of outrage. Maybe no-one listened to book programmes on local radio in the 70s. I recently discussed the incident again with Derek Robinson. Chuckling while at the same time defending his protagonist, he said: 'I think Alan got it wrong. The book is still in print, you know.'

The undeniable fact is that Gibson did leave himself open to accusations of double-standards. His Baptist and Methodist roots caused him visibly to recoil from blasphemy and bad language. A traffic officer or two and a desk sergeant, in the station where he had been once brought in disgrace and disarray, might arch their brows, however, at such a notion. His attitude to expletives was the source of a much-quoted, and some of us would suggest, hilarious incident in the Hove press box. The exchanges and good-natured barbs had been plentiful. Gibson, briefly in residence, no doubt because he wanted to ascertain an esoteric Sussex fact or borrow the local freelance's phone, could contain himself no longer. 'I've only been in this box a short time and already I've heard the f-word used 13 times. I can't stand the language being debased any more and I've no wish to stay.' He said it with donnish bombast. One of the regional cricket reporters bristled as he swung round to confront the patronising Head. 'Don't forget to shut the effing door as you leave – and don't vandalise the trains on the effing way home.' Touché.

Gibson rejected cliché, sentimentality and what he perceived as sham. Maybe he inwardly enjoyed some of the contradictions that he generated within his own character. He could be acidulous, the calculated curmudgeon. But he could just as easily be the bar-room luminary, enlightening every conversation with insights or quotations that were utterly beyond most of us. He could be congenial, a stimulating companion, chivalrous and charming. One could often detect angst in the dregs of his glass.

John Arlott, so helpful to him in his early years of sports broadcasting, remained a good friend and claimed Alan was the most amusing sports reporter of his day. John Woodcock was another loyal friend. To Alan, John was always 'The Sage of Longparish'; he conferred such titles in profusion and genuine affection. Some of the deep friendships went back to Oxford, among them his with the clerical brother of Dickie Dodds, the Essex batsman. Dickie's brother had also been to Taunton School. Alan much liked the family; as a lay preacher after he had left Oxford, he was invited to give the address at the Anglican church where the brothers' father was the vicar. There were many lively discussions on religion. Dickie, famed for the speed with which he attractively assembled his runs, an odd transformation from his earlier studied caution at the crease, is a well-known supporter of Moral Rearmament. Some aspects, but not too many, found favour with Gibson. He was critical of others, among them the method, influenced by MR, by which Dickie chose his wife, based on a fleeting prayer, a Somerset batsman's swipe off a bad ball and a catch in the outfield by the Essex man of God. Gibson enjoyed the cut-and-thrust of religious debate, just as he enjoyed writing of Dodds' exhilarating innings. 'He was always pulling my leg. Unlike him, I left school at 16 and was much cheered when he gave a glowing review to a coaching book of mine, saying it was "grammatically correct and limpidly clear",' Dickie said.

It isn't easy to be specific about when the physical decline began. There had been so many bouts of depression and caverns of introspection, so many suicide threats, so much disquieting evidence that it was impossible to lead a normal life with him. The second family had moved to High Littleton, a village not far from Bath, where he appeared to spend nearly as much time in The Star as at his home, the appositely though deceptively named Old Market Tavern. If he was taking the country bus into Bath in mid-morning, he liked to nip into The Star for a whisky "to steady himself down for the day ahead". In truth, he never had too much money, and it was just as well a succession of landlords were surprisingly tolerant over his mounting bar debts. He did his best to honour them. But he was a local celebrity, after all, and he could summon up reserves of charm when the back trouser pocket was light.

Rosemary, his second wife had once worked in the Features Department of the BBC and was, in his own words, used to temperamental broadcasters. Their marriage and honeymoon – of necessary improvisation – which featured the bride's accidental leaving of her travelling bag at Waterloo station and the bridegroom's fractured ankle, was sheer Feydeau. In his way Alan much loved her, though later he too easily ignored her and her needs. His affection for his children from the marriage, Adam and Felicity, was genuine without ever being demonstrative. He found it difficult to show his emotions. When not at the pub, he was inclined to shut himself away with his books. The children – and it was probably harder for Felicity – were left to ponder the nature of their parents' disintegrating relationship. Adam was sent to Wellington School, in Somerset; Felicity went through the state system. Both are now teachers.

'There was always an assumption that we'd be successful academically,' said Adam. 'The other two sons had gone to Oxford and Queen's College. It was the saddest day of my life when I visited my father in hospital to tell him

I hadn't got in. I think I was very close but I did a bad interview. I can still see my father's tear-filled eyes. There was a pause before he spoke.'

'It's my fault,' he said poignantly.

Alan was apt to withdraw from the responsibilities of fatherhood while Rosemary resiliently ran the home and handled the tantrums. 'Dad could still be very strict – he had a hell of a temper.' Alan did few of the normal domestic things. He never sat with the family, in the conventional sense, to watch the television, for instance; in fact, he steadfastly refused to look at what he called "the one-eyed god". One rare exception was during a holiday in a St Ives hotel. 'We persuaded him, I don't know how, to watch *Time and the Conways*.' It must have been a reluctant concession to Priestley, a fellow Yorkshireman.

Because of Alan's flaws, moods and erratic lifestyle, the marriage was clearly not going to work. Rosemary, who had admired him so much as a broadcaster and longed for a regulated and civilised married life, was increasingly disillusioned. She threatened him with divorce but he blithely refused to believe it would ever happen. On the day the papers were served, Adam went into Alan's study in filial loyalty to offer some sympathy.

'She doesn't mean it, Adam. She's only going through the motions to frighten me.'

Adam knew differently. 'I felt quite awful. Mother had discussed it with me and even asked me what I thought. It seemed to me that a mixture of his usual self-confidence and alcohol had insulated my father against such a possibility, understandable though it was.'

When Alan realised in abject dismay the marriage was over, he went to pieces. There was another attempt on his life with an overdose. Older son Anthony found him in time and phoned for the ambulance. In turn Alan was taken to a specialist centre for drying-out at Weston-super-Mare. But that kind of therapy found no favours with him. He called a taxi and walked out, turning up, to everyone's surprise, at High Littleton again, and expecting Rosemary to pay the fare.

Much kindly and practical advice was offered to the disconsolate, confused and often bad-tempered Gibson. He agreed to take the lease on a flat in Queen's Court, Clifton, Bristol, very near to one of his previous homes, in the vain hope that rediscovered glimpses of a happier past might work. Instead, it was a disaster. 'My father lived in a state of unimaginable squalor and desolation. Conditions were so bad that he was removed to the Bristol Royal Infirmary and from there to Ham Green Hospital, where he was treated for his alcoholism and appeared to make a remarkable recovery,' Anthony said.

Alan accepted that it was time for some self-examination of his receding life and a positive attempt to pick up some of the damaged, creative threads of a career which had been wantonly discarded. Anthony, doing his best to disguise his own considerable apprehension, told his father he was still capable of writing on cricket for a living. *The Times*, which had basked in the compliments of those readers who knew nothing of his demons, had finally despaired after much patience, and taken him off the cricket circuit. Now they agreed to give him some more matches and to reserve judgment.

It was a last chance. Anthony found his father another flat in Taunton; he detected signs, real or imagined, of renewed purpose and excitement for the game they both liked so much. And, yes, there was the day he drove Alan to Taunton station and put him safely on the train.

With a half smile, he said: 'Whatever you do, father, don't get drunk.'

Alan said: 'Bye, Ants.' Almost in the same breath, he turned to a fellow passenger and loudly asked: 'Where's the buffet car and the bar?'

He was pointedly telling his well-intentioned son that he was not prepared to be dictated to. He made sure he was overheard. It revealed a cussed, insensitive streak.

In fact, the two saw plenty of each other. And Alan needed to be constantly bullied. He listened to and appeared to be accepting wise counsel with good grace. Then he promptly ignored it. Anthony, a busy man himself, lived fairly close at hand. He ferried his father around and often phoned his copy, privately marvelling at the surviving style, the sentence construction, the clarity of meaning, the sly jokes. 'How does Dad do it?' he asked himself recurrently. 'He's been knocking back the doubles all day.'

The whisky bottle was indeed once more winning the brutal battle. Alan became unreliable, missing a few deadlines, causing apoplexy to members of his paper's sports desk who were never completely confident about his whereabouts. Yet, as his son had noted, the quality of his writing during that slightly cosmetic journalistic comeback was high. He remained readable, entertaining and as idiosyncratic as ever. Alas, there was only so much that *The Times* could take.

One day, while he briefly made his return to the cricket writers' rota, he spent some time with me in the beer tent at Bath, at a time of the annual festival. I couldn't quite determine whether he'd filed his copy but professional duties were, he quickly made clear, not on his conversational agenda. He was well into his cups and pleasantly intimate. Repeatedly, without any prompting on my part to discuss his marital misery, he said: 'I knew when I lost Rosie, you know, that I'd never be able to write another thing. I'm lost. Written-out.'

He wasn't trying to shift any of the blame on her – that would have been quite unfair – but he became engulfed in self-pity after his second divorce. 'I think he believed that, if he degraded himself sufficiently, Rosie would arrive to rescue him. Self-destruction with a purpose,' Anthony said. That was, however, a sad episode in the Bath beer tent, and it kept coming back to me.

In the following years of ghastly decline, and frustration for those who tried to help, he stayed in six or seven residential and nursing homes in the Taunton area, 'most of which he either walked out of, or was thrown out of'. Several of those homes did their best to provide him with proper food and a homely environment. His son used to give him pocket money which he rapidly disposed of at the bar of "The Cottage" and other local pubs. Good, loyal friends like John Woodcock and an ex-teacher, Richard Walsh, called to cheer him up or take him for a ride. One journalistic chum bought a raincoat and discreetly left it for Alan.

At one point, Anthony edited a collection of Alan's essays, snippets, BBC scripts, philosophical asides and thoughts on lore and literature. The paperback, *West Country Treasury*, was published and well-received. They even had a book launch. 'I did it to give my father something to do. They were mostly reprints and I got them typed up at work. It was good for him and he enjoyed it.'

Alan Gibson with son Anthony at the launch of 'West Country Treasury'

But Alan's appearance started to change alarmingly. The old cerebral jauntiness and physical presence had gone. He was now gaunt and cadaverous. His eyes were sunken and the wispy, unruly hair reminding one of an impotent figure from a Chekovian tragedy. At times he was put in a taxi, by someone at the residential home, to be driven to the county ground in Taunton which had, after all, been his favourite venue. That was where I saw him last, predictably in the Stragglers' Bar, back to the play, unseeing eyes drifting along the lines of an old classic. The pages were stained and stuck together, the print almost illegible. He had nothing to say, apart from mumbling that cricket meant nothing to him and he didn't know why he was there. For nearly an hour we sat in awkward silence; earlier gentle questions from me had earned no response. He was in a wheelchair and twice I pushed him to the lavatory. There was a cruel absence of dignity about the little scene. Members nudged each other. 'That Alan Gibson?'

No it wasn't. Alan Gibson was a scholar of some standing, quite a celebrity, a well respected man who knew more about Defoe, Hazlitt, and the Romantics, about God and Gladstone and ... Sammy Woods than all of them put together.

This was a skeleton within whom, I suspected, the mind still ticked frenziedly and agonisingly. But the spark and fervour of Liberalism had gone for good. Worse, it appeared, so had his faith. That fiery dissenter's zeal, which once he manifested from country pulpits in Devon, had been abandoned. He had rejected his God, his life.

It made me think once more of Olwen's words: 'He used to go round the chapels near Totnes in his formal black Non-Conformist suit in the days before we were married and he hadn't long come down from Oxford. He was such a passionate preacher, just from a few notes. But he had this tremendous knowledge – many of the books in his enormous library were on theology ... And what a fine political speaker he was. Old-style oratory, plenty of emotion. It's what they call charismatic nowadays.'

And I remembered vividly the broadcaster: the assertive perfectly modulated voice, the leisurely, meaningful pace, the canny pauses to gain maximum effect from an original, descriptive phrase, the wit that was never too far away, the withering piece of reportage when a batsman erred.

Such images had nothing to do with the sunken, silent, embittered man who dribbled in his whisky glass and pretended he was still reading an erudite tome.

Gibson was to me – and many others – infuriating and immensely kind. He was a towering intellectual, ready to let you know if you tended to get above your station. He could show-off a little with his abstruse classical allusions. Academia, from which he was never alienated in spirit, was allowed to become on occasions a trifle too intrusive.

'He was' said Anthony, 'a daunting figure intellectually. He had this extraordinary memory and could, for example, recall in detail the plot of a play he'd seen for the first time thirty or forty years before – and the cast list. It was wonderful to have a father so highly regarded and well known, something that did my street-cred no harm at all. But that exceptional intellect of his left me feeling inferior, knowing I could never live up to it.'

Adam, a younger son from a different marriage, was to say virtually the same to me. Their honest, analytical judgment didn't obscure the measure of their awe or, in the case of all the children, their admiration.

Amid the emotional undulation of his gifted, tormented and wayward life, Alan was a person of compassion. This was evident when he spoke at the memorial service for Sir Neville Cardus, and again at the service for the Somerset batsman, Harold Gimblett, who committed suicide at the age of 63.

The pews at St James's Church in Taunton, just a fine-leg distance from the county ground, were packed with players and supporters. Alan climbed the steps of the pulpit and apologised for becoming personal. This was what he started by saying:

> Fifteen years ago I was in a mental hospital after failing to kill myself. Many friends wrote to me, sympathising at that difficult time. The most understanding letter and the wisest advice came from Harold. As a result of that, we would sometimes in later years talk, not morbidly, about the problems of people such as us, beset by bouts of depression, often quite irrational. Experience of mental illness, he insisted, should be used to help others. He worked in recent years for the Samaritans and I'm sure he did it very well.

It was my privileged turn to say a few words at Alan's funeral service in Taunton Baptist Church in April 1997. Anthony had asked me; we agreed it should be informal, anecdotal and celebratory. In the congregation were pockets of academics, some from his Oxford days, along with former BBC producers, cricketers and cricket writers. The two ex-wives were there with their children. It was not a solemn address; nor was it in any sense irreligious. I tried to make it clear, with as much tact as the occasion demanded, that he was no saint. He would, I hope, have approved of that.

After the service we went along to the county ground for our cups of tea and ritualistic exchanges of reminiscence. It was an upbeat wake. The setting couldn't have been better.

Adam, whom I met there for the first time, wrote to me afterwards. "The memories you evoked have prompted many recollections in all his children – some funny, some sad, some maddening, some proud – but all touching and characteristic of the incredible man who was our father. Having seen his gradual physical decline, it is very easy for me to lose sight of some of the most important things about him ... I feel a great deal of pride, humour and sympathy in my love and grieving for him."

He died, according to the certificate, from a chest infection at the age of 73. The obituaries in the broadsheets and regional papers were long and generous. I was asked to do one for *The Guardian*, one of the papers for whom Alan used to write on cricket and rugby. It was long, affectionate and shied away from hagiography.

A short time after, I received a letter from Alan's former Test match and BBC colleague, Don Mosey, "The Alderman" as he was dubbed, a no-nonsense Yorkshireman who set high standards, had no time for frivolity and said he was appalled by the excess of public-school accents in the box. His bluntness was part of his appeal and I'd have been disappointed not to discover an unequivocal blast at his old employers.

I was absolutely furious that the BBC took the trouble to ring Fred Trueman to tell him of Alan's death but no-one thought of telling me. Fred barely knew the man; I had been associated with him on a very friendly basis for nearly 40 years.

Even so, he gave me one or two nasty turns. At Sheffield in the late 60s when I was a pretty junior figure at the BBC and producer of Yorkshire v the Indian touring team, Alan arrived for commentary very much the worse for wear – at 12 noon! To make matters worse, his co-commentator, an Anglo-Indian was in an even more lamentable state. It later transpired that they had "gone for a drink" with Norman Yardley after the previous day's play and had drunk the night away, even pausing for an additional pint on their way through the Bramall Lane bar to the commentary box the following morning.

To use that well-known phrase, "the BBC switchboard was flooded with complaints". Back in Bristol, sports producer Tony Smith got almost as many as London received. And I was blamed for allowing Alan to broadcast.

By 1975, Cliff Morgan was in charge in London and at the meeting where we sorted out Test match commentators for the season, he opposed the use of Alan. Tony and I insisted, however, and Cliff told me grimly: "Upon your head be it." When, on the Monday night of the Test, Alan had made a bit of a mess of things, Cliff phoned me: "He doesn't broadcast tomorrow, see. I don't care what you have to do." And overnight, the 'Friends of George Davis' dug up the Headingley pitch!

Nevertheless I remained a friend and admirer of Alan. I insisted that he should script and present the BBC's tribute to John Arlott after his retirement in 1980. In the course of the recording, in Bristol, Alan suggested we should adjourn for what he called a little refreshment. I positively snarled at him "Not until we've got the programme in the can." And we both laughed.

If only there had been more laughter.

His departure from the Test match panel was discreetly done. The BBC knew how upset he would be so decided, considerate in their psychology, to send him no official letter. Those of his employers who had listened to that final broadcast from Leeds, exchanging phone calls even as he stumbled over his words, were prepared however to take no more risks.

Alan Gibson accepted that his dismissal was self-induced. 'But the umpire's finger went up too quickly,' he was to say with a touching innocence.

Let it be openly admitted. Those of us, whose love of cricket borders on barmy obsession, have never progressed in spirit far from the second form. We wallow in the game's idiotic glossary, its risible rituals and the habitual tang of linseed oil. The unspoken confidences we share go beyond the sporting, almost to the Masonic. We're a secret society with bronzed faces and clear eyes that carry a thousand dreams of players and matches that mostly we only pretended we saw.

It isn't enough for us to play and score negligible runs, to watch from behind the bowler's arm, to sit with our sandwich boxes on the cover boundary and field the ball from Hammond in a heady joy of perpetuation. We are also cursed with rampant, discursive imaginations that ceaselessly take us down quirky, meaningless by-ways. Just as when we once scribbled on the inside back covers of our school exercise books, forging Test-playing heroes' signatures, so we continue to invent absurd, childish games about our cricketers, past and present.

What other deranged segment of the human race, dons as well as dullards, would challenge our wayward intellectual faculties by devising whole teams whose surnames bear an approximation, say, to the timeless possessions of our sylvan heritage or maybe even our anatomical parts? A whimsically compiled side of Adonis-like amateurs, virginally fresh from their pre-war public schools; or, more to my liking, eleven merry-eyed professionals renowned for their boozing? Teams of first class cricketers who went on to become doctors or lawyers? Ugly teams, lofty teams, bad tempered teams? It was something to do, to laugh about and argue over while the rain was coming down.

Boundary historians can be insufferably punctilious. It isn't enough for them to recall an occasional vacation player who used to turn up in August at the expense of malleable pros with twice as much ability. The name is enunciated with show-off solemnity, along with all three initials. The degree of emphasis suggests that the initials are of more importance. As if we really cared.

I'm not at all certain that Siegfried Sassoon was a pedant in such matters. In earlier research, however, I was to discover his propensity for clothing old-style amateurs in the full dress of their initials, as if they were socially naked without them. Not that the habit lacked humour. I have told previously of the occasion that Mad Jack, "the Squire of Heytesbury", was having a meal with friends and a player or two after a match at Fenner's. A nervous waiter spilled soup down the front of the Cambridge 12th man. 'Oh, Christ!' was one spontaneous reaction of horror. Sassoon, calm as ever, quickly eased the tension. 'Let me see, now. Christ J, wasn't it?'

Initials mean rather less now, receding in distinction with the changing times. Some Solent sages contend that three initials are the statutory requirements for captaincy of Hampshire. It isn't quite true, of course. Robin Smith made do with two. The fact is that our silly word games still go on. We can come up with a whole team of eggheads – led by Mike Brearley – during our mental doodles in the tea interval. In mischievous mood and within the confines of the press box, we have also been known to speculate good naturedly over sexual proclivities. But one particular challenge is apt to leave us with a depleted side.

'Go on, compile a list of Lefties.' It should be easy enough. Statistically, with the law of averages, you would think the dressing rooms reverberated in the days of New Labour to the rumbles of modestly radical pronouncements. Not so. County cricket, and that is particularly true of the last forty years, is predominantly right-wing. One winces, not just *Guardian* pinkos like myself, at some of the reactionary views expressed with an air of unequivocal finality. This has been the case with many of the older players; the young ones don't really care. Did they ever?

Decades ago, Surrey had some fearful rows over wages. Threats were real enough from intrepid pros, some clearly with barrack-room aggression and political thoughts that dovetailed with emergent socialistic notions. Charlie Parker, a farm labourer's son, studied the Russian Revolution and had no qualms about quoting Marxism as well as biblical passages to his doting Gloucestershire team-mates. Gloucester's Bomber Wells also possessed a proud radical spirit. Somerset was the county of my birth and heart. One idol, Bill Andrews used to tell me how he was made to remove a leaflet supporting Labour from his front window. Another idol, Harold Gimblett, who went to a minor public school and whose family hailed from the Tory heartlands of West Somerset, Jack White's red-soiled territory, came to hate the country's establishment and switched from Right to Left. Peter Roebuck seemed fervently Labour at one time; but then his personal political manifesto could, it seemed to me, oscillate abruptly, even if never beyond the halfway line. Several of his university contemporaries, while not coming overtly out of the closet, revealed scant allegiance to doctrines of the Conservative Party. One fast bowler, proud of his coal-mining forebears, used to tell me he thought he was the only Labour supporter in the Derbyshire dressing room; he appeared noticeably to mellow after that.

Tom Cartwright never mellowed. He was born in a miner's cottage on the edge of Coventry. There was no running water, no obvious accepted upward social pattern for the future. Tom was taken down the pit to be shown what it was like; he often travelled on the colliers' bus, sitting next to men with their blue coal scars. He listened to the miners' voices and, still in his boyhood, aligned himself in spirit with their needs and their valid grievances.

As an apprentice county cricketer he worked for several winters on the assembly line in the car industry. He was conscious of the mood of apprehension, the division between management and workers. He was an uneasy observer of the wholesale redundancies. 'I saw grown men crying. I stood with my father in the dole queue when it was seven or eight deep across the pavement in Coventry. What I saw happening left a deep impression on me and it would never disappear. I was confronted by another facet of life.'

Young Tom's character was being shaped. He was aware that the canvas was broader than cricket. Some aspects of mining and factory existence were naggingly disturbing to him. He was caught up in working-class disquiet and frustration. His experiences on the factory floor, however brief, were to mould the man. He told himself he'd not be manipulated or exploited. Like his father before him, he despised those who fawned. It made him defensive and, some on the committees at Edgbaston and Taunton contended, bloody-minded. He was obsessed with a sense of justice – for himself as much as his fellow players. Altogether too much of a barrack-room lawyer for us, said one Somerset official.

That was an excessive generalisation. It ignored the rigid integrity of the man.

He had a wary regard for authority and was too fluent in argument for some of the 'amateurs' and bystanders who populated cricket's committee retreats. Their ignorance of man management and suspect qualifications for being there at all made him bristle. As Vic Marks put it: "Tom was no lover of the establishment *per se*."

Tom, Coach of the Year, with wife Joan and son Jeremy

Ironically, as the national coach in Wales, he has now become a cherished member of the Welsh sporting establishment. He was equally embraced by being made, in the New Year Honours of 2000, an MBE and, by receiving from Princess Anne the Dyson Award, to enter the National Foundation Hall of Fame. This dual recognition touched him, though he considered it reflected the team around him. On his idealistic initiative, however, cricket had been restructured and stimulated round the by-ways of the Principality. Much latent talent has been unearthed; some has found its way to Sophia Gardens.

Nothing has shaken me from my view that he is the finest cricket coach in Britain. Maybe England should have used him more. He has the technical answer – and the human one. He can be perverse and contrary when he feels the coaching edicts are taking us in the wrong direction. But the boys who come to play their fledgling shots or listen to his wisdom, dote on his words. And the words, in a voice that continues to reveal faintly the vowels of the Midlands, are plentiful. He can talk incessantly about cricket: quietly, sensibly, persuasively.

In 1975 I was asked to edit a brochure to commemorate Somerset's centenary year. Cartwright was then the county coach and I went to Mike Brearley for an evaluation of someone as yet not well known in the West Country. This is part of what he wrote:

> Tom Cartwright, of all the cricketers I know, comes closest to the ideal craftsman. He is, I'd say, the best medium pace bowler in cricket today.
>
> In addition, he is a great thinker – and talker – about the game.
>
> He has strong, clear views about behaviour and standards on and off the field. He has no time for misguided or misused authority and is contemptuous of fawning and hypocrisy. His knowledge of cricket and people is invaluable to him as a coach.
>
> Somerset did well to get Brian Close; they were even more shrewd in persuading Cartwright. In case this sounds too good to be true, I would add that Tom's forthrightness can get close to stubbornness. And he does occasionally feel that umpires can't tell a straight ball when they see one.
>
> He is an excellent coach. He's one of the few people I would travel to see for help in my own cricket. He knows very well that no form of teaching can be successful if it is merely technical or simply rule-guided. Somerset's emergence over the last few years owes a great deal to him.

My first casual acquaintance with him was when he arrived at Taunton in 1970. I enjoyed watching that leap of his on delivery. He didn't need the new ball and I chuckled to myself as established batsmen agonised in trying to take runs off him. I moved behind his arm, whichever end he was bowling, trying to discern the measure of movement off that seemingly amiable pace. Batsmen eventually became exasperated and sacrificed their wicket with uncharacteristically reckless shots. 'Too bloody negative, that's the trouble with Cartwright,' they would bellow to no one in particular as they hurled bats vaguely in the direction of their coffins. This reaction, with which he was only too familiar, irritated him. Who last saw him bowl to a defensive field, he would ask? His method of bowling was to him a psychological battle; a ploy was the word he most used.

As a sports reporter covering the West Country for an evening paper in those days, in daily contact with club and individual players, the feed-back to Cartwright's skills as a coach was significant. One player said Tom had a tendency to favourites, impatient with those whose attention was inclined to stray. Another found him if anything too demanding for a county where historically the cricketers were not always possessed of a competitive nature and preferred an easy-going session in the nets. Almost all of them found him fundamentally paternal. At that time, Somerset's 2nd XI was laden with promise, a goodly proportion nurtured at Millfield. Cartwright was much encouraged by his raw material. He was living at Wells and loving the gentle, ecclesiastical calm of the small city. He had his family around him, and was as happy and relaxed as he'd even been.

His star pupil was Ian Botham. It might have seemed an unlikely alliance of master and pupil. Botham was young, noisy, self-confident. He'd gone off to Lord's where the coach Len Muncer didn't always know what to make of him, largely because he went on doing things determinedly his own way. He had rather too many opinions for a 16-year-old. He was knocking back pints of beer with the macho unconcern of a brawny building site labourer (which he'd been for a few months back in Yeovil). Cartwright had seen, and secretly admired, enough stroppy but spunky workers back on the assembly-line. He took to Botham. 'Both' interestingly never implied he was already a self-sufficient young cricketer, in the presence of Cartwright. They maintained an easy and warm relationship.

Sometimes it was suggested that Tom taught him how to bowl. 'And, in a way, it was probably true. I also allowed him to develop in a completely natural manner. For his part he had the most receptive ability to absorb quickly. He was physically strong and virile, and it was like dealing with an adult. I didn't try to curb or over-coach him. He took criticism and didn't answer back.'

Cartwright's first glimpse of Botham had been in a class of 15-year-olds, being run at Millfield by Bill Andrews, the former Somerset coach. There were 30 or so boys hitting tennis balls, and it was the firm-muscled lad from Yeovil who stood out. Tom was soon to be appointed the county's player-coach. He was surrounded by youthful talent: Roebuck, Slocombe, Marks, Lloyds, Denning, Jennings, Gard. 'I've seen your batting. But what about your bowling, Ian?' Botham shrugged and said it was being treated as a joke. Cartwright asked him if he was prepared to work at it; the response was immediate. The pupil learnt how to swing the ball both ways in a matter of weeks. He learnt the secrets of seam, how to use his body as much as his arms. And he was discouraged from bowling too fast.

Here was, of course, exceptional potential. Cartwright was not a man to parade his emotions and enthusiasms. Midlanders seldom are. But he inherently knew that the young Botham, who pretended all he wanted to do was play for Chelsea, could be a Test cricketer one day. It has been said he was lucky Cartwright was around to augment the generous natural gifts with the technical refinements. 'I should say I was equally lucky that Ian was around for me.'

In his early days as a county cricketer, Botham was always being urged to bowl faster. Cartwright, sagacious to a degree, shook his head. He considered it a compliment when observers claimed that Somerset's new young bowling discovery had consciously copied the style and technique of Tom. Several of Both's playing contemporaries told me how he would announce: 'I've decided to bowl my Tom Cartwrights today'. The run-up would be adjusted: and the similarity in action was uncanny.

It is hard to imagine that many can have studied the mechanics of bowling more profoundly than Cartwright. When he talks of lateral movement, he gives his treatise an almost poetic quality. His words don't come in rigid prosaic fashion as if from a coaching manual. They arrive in an enthusiastic surge, coloured by personal experience and the lingering images of a thousand classes in county grounds and school halls. He's part instructor, part philosopher. 'Only two things I was really any good at, you know,' he tells you. 'Playing the game and coaching others to play it.'

He started playing it seriously from the age of eleven. That was when he came under the influence of one of the teachers, Eddie Branson, a Yorkshireman just back from the war. The master's passion for cricket was quickly conveyed to Tom, who was still only eleven when Mr Branson selected him for the Coventry Schools' Under-14 side. As an annual treat, the master took the boys to Edgbaston to watch some county cricket. While still at school, Tom did the double; by the age of sixteen, he was a Warwickshire prospect. It had been a predetermined route.

Any distinct ambitions as a bowler, however, seemed sparingly recognised. He looked around, with the wary eyes of a surprisingly canny teenager, and worked out that the county already had nine seamers. 'What chance did I have? I reckoned I would need to make my way as a batsman.'

If Mr Branson was his first mentor, Warwickshire's Tiger Smith was the second and greatest of all. Young Cartwright never changed his opinion that Tiger was the best coach in the world. 'He had three daughters and I think I was the son he never had. He was tough, as you'd expect from a Midlands heavyweight boxer, but was always particularly kind and helpful to me. He told me he'd make me – or break me.'

Tiger devoted hours to Tom's progress, in the Edgbaston nets. From him, the young frustrated all-rounder acquired much of the cricketing knowledge, never fanciful or verging far from common sense, that he gratefully retained and built on.

He had joined Warwickshire in 1952. He watched and listened avidly for seven years; more or less as he had feared, there was meagre scope for bowling at first team level. Pragmatically he got on with his batting, with such resolve that he scored 210 against Middlesex at Nuneaton in 1962. By then, his bowling was no longer submerged beneath the surfeit of Edgbaston seam. That same year he did the double, and took 8-39 against Somerset at Weston-super-Mare, on the Clarence Park ground where once children encroached on the outfield to dig sandcastles. Not that Cartwright ever needed artificial aids.

Maybe this is the moment to get the statistics out of the way. They didn't mean a great deal to him; he was a team man. The mental battle with a fine batsman, often won by Tom as he wickedly hit the seam, invariably gave him more pleasure than running through a succession of tailenders with perfunctory efficiency.

Those career records, then. He played for Warwickshire from 1952-69 and Somerset from 1970-76. There followed seven token appearances for Glamorgan. In all he scored 13,710 runs at 32.7 and took 1,536 wickets; he also held onto 332 catches, many at slip or close to the wicket. Three times he topped 1000 runs in a season, eight times he took more than 100 wickets. He made five appearances for England, inadequate recognition, and we shall come to that later.

Tom Cartwright batting against Middlesex, 1961
John Murray is the wicket-keeper, Fred Titmus at slip

The county debut had been noteworthy. For the last match of the 1952 summer, Warwickshire went to Trent Bridge and, because he'd been showing such promise in the 2nd XI and no doubt on the strong recommendation of Tiger Smith, Cartwright was brought into the side. No question of being given a bowl, but to his surprise he was number four in the order. He justified his unlikely and elevated position by scoring 82 in the first innings and 22 not out in the second. It earned him headlines back in the Birmingham and Coventry papers.

Wisden said that the game produced some of the best cricket seen at Nottingham that season. Reg Simpson, full of graceful stroke-play and with all the relaxation that often comes as the season ends, scored a double hundred. It took him no more than four hours. Young Cartwright was just as long over his 82 but it was studiously made, without the sign of a flaw. There was much praise from both sides. 'I shouldn't try to sweep too much,' said a paternal Joe Hardstaff. Kindly words to youthful opponents were once freely given by all but the game's few well-known curmudgeons. Why did cricket's generous heart disappear?

His progress as a batsman was maintained. The next year he found himself at times opening the Warwickshire innings with Fred Gardner. Still only seventeen, he went to the Oval, where an extraordinary match was over in a day. Surrey won by an innings, Alec Bedser ended with a dozen wickets, and Jim Laker performed the hat-trick. The pitch was described in the records as 'treacherous' and Bedser had difficulty obtaining a proper foothold. He simply cut down his pace and attacked the leg stump. Twenty nine wickets fell in the day and not a single Warwickshire batsman was bowled. As one remembered so well, Surrey's catching could be magnificent and so adept that it appeared like an optical illusion. 'An extraordinary day's cricket – and what an experience for someone like me, just coming into the game.'

Years later, when with Somerset, Cartwright took part in a game with Shropshire which was also over in a day. 'Am I,' he's inclined to joke, 'the only cricketer to have been in a county championship and Minor Counties match decided in a day?'

In the years with Warwickshire that followed, he seemed to do well against Somerset. Once he did the hat-trick at Edgbaston. He scored a century against them, too, though only through the goodness of Colin McCool's heart. Tom was on 97 and his county needed one run to win. McCool looked up at the scoreboard and then tossed down a full toss on the leg side. 'Go on, hit it for four,' he shouted. The generosity of a fellow pro wasn't forgotten. 'I was delighted he felt my innings was worthy of that kind of gesture. As we came off the field, Colin came up to me and said I deserved it.' Another example of different days, this time from a naturally competitive Aussie.

Why no more than five Tests? Some argued that he looked too innocuous and would be taken apart by great international batsmen. That was a pre-judgment that he lived with, knowing it – as did many domestic batters who ritualistically perished in their annual duels with him – to be superficial and untrue. The old prejudices about him being too much of a negative bowler, another fallacy, had the habit of resurfacing at untimely moments when Test teams were being selected.

In his Tests he played under Ted Dexter and Mike Smith. His bowling figures were comparatively modest but never bad; in the case of Trent Bridge, the second Test against South Africa in 1965, he was by some distance the best bowler we had. The conditions were heavy and overcast. Cartwright exploited them marvellously to take 6-94. His figures might have been even better but for wretched luck. He had taken four wickets, after gaining his first two without conceding a run. Then he threw himself forward for a return catch.

'The ball hit my thumb and I knew at once I was in trouble. I got hold of the thumb and pulled it back. But it turned out to be a double fracture and I didn't bowl in the second innings. The thumb is so important, the rudder if you like, for swing bowling.'

South Africa won the match – and in effect the series – by 94 runs. The Pollock brothers had a wonderful Test. Graeme made 125 in an exquisite innings that is still talked about; Peter took five wickets in each innings.

He went on the MCC tour of South Africa in 1964-65 and saw enough of the political regime to be uncomfortable. But his injury was genuine when he withdrew from the Test party to go there in 1968-69. His announced replacement was Basil D'Oliveira – and the outcome was the cessation of Test matches with the Republic until new attitudes belatedly prevailed. The tour was cancelled and we can only speculate that Cartwright, even if fit, would have been emotionally inhibited as a member of the party.

Yes, as we have reflected, he was bloody-minded. In analytical enclaves with this writer, he admitted it. 'I supported causes when I felt I needed to. It didn't always do me much good.'

He remains a sensitive man. His wife is Welsh, an ex-teacher. The family has always been the nub of his life, 'especially babies' he adds with self-conscious retrospection. He lives contentedly in Neath, motors the valleys and the hilltop Welsh-speaking villages: always with a bat and a few cricket balls in the boot of his car. He likes the warmth and compact humanity of simple Welsh life. So many of the pits are now no more than receding scars on the sides of every valley. Nearly every day he listens to mining memories that evoke his own early rides on the colliers' buses just outside Coventry. His eyes are also apt to sparkle rather like those of an old-style cloth-cap union leader intent on better times. I saw it for myself at a lovely cricket ground in the Neath Valley in the summer of 1995. Exactly 25 years after the all-white South African cricket tour to this country was stopped, we had the first black South African side to tour here and play in Wales, at Ynysygerwyn.

Controversy has not easily passed Cartwright by. There were rumbles of disaffection, from both parties, when he left Warwickshire and then Somerset.

His departure from Warwickshire came after 18 years. He was thinking of other options like coaching and was ready to move on. It was hardly a secret. Leicestershire, for instance, were prepared to offer him £600 more than he was getting at Edgbaston. 'People were writing in, asking me to stay. All I wanted was to slip away quietly. The county were saying I was looking for more money and that was ludicrous. While I was on holiday in Corfu, they put out a statement that I'd retired from cricket. Not quite true – I'd resigned.'

Some of the politics weren't pleasant. He was ready for a complete break. Colin Atkinson offered him a coaching job at Millfield and then he joined Somerset. 'I loved the West Country and in many ways would like to live there now. The countryside appealed to me, the people and the pace of life. As for Taunton, it's still a shire ground … you get held up by tractors on the way to work. Lovely. So many county grounds have lost what they're meant to be.' More evidence of the sensitivity within that paradoxical Cartwright persona.

He played 101 matches for Somerset and coached countless boys. He scored a hundred at Leyton and took more than 400 wickets, including eight in an innings at Chesterfield. It is true to say that not every committee member warmed to him. 'Too bloody independent. Always wants his own way,' it would be observed with feudal disdain.

The parting was, as we say in the best journalistic circles, acrimonious. It was highly dramatic, too – with hurtful exchanges and raised voices. One withering scene with the then chairman of Somerset, Herbie Hoskins, normally an amiable, unworldly farmer-figure from the village of Sparkford in South Somerset, took place in the Gents at Clarence Park, during the Weston-super-Mare festival.

Cartwright had been badly injured, on the head and shoulder, when he collided at full speed with the Sussex player, John Spencer. Married with a young family, he argued that he couldn't jeopardise his future by playing again that season. But he did agree to lead the 2nd XI against Shropshire at Bath. The county officials noted that he bowled in one innings and took six wickets. When the next day he went to watch the championship match at Weston, he was told he was needed for the Sunday fixture.

A letter had already been received by him, telling him his employment as coach was coming to an end. It looked as though his links with Somerset were being curtailed. But a lavatory was hardly the most salubrious of settings for the heated dualogue. 'You're playing, Tom. We've talked to the doctor and our advice is that you are fit.'

'Taking the word of a paediatrician, are you?' was Cartwright's rejoinder, tinged with sarcasm. He was stubborn and angry, upset that his own assessment of fitness was not believed. There was committee talk of his letting the team down. A quorum was gathered for an improvised committee meeting at Weston. Later he was handed an envelope by the secretary, Roy Stevens, who then disappeared 'in a cloud of dust as he headed for his car'. The note told Cartwright that he was being suspended and should not set foot on a Somerset ground again. He was also paid up till the end of the season. 'Brian Close said it was quite outrageous. He and the players wanted me to join them for the next county match in Bristol, but I told them I'd been ordered to stay away.'

That was the end of his Somerset cricket and the cherished residency at Wells. He'd always got on well with Close, himself acutely out of love with Yorkshire at the time and brought to the West Country to toughen the same rustic fibre. 'I found Closey quite brilliant. We thought the same way about how the game should be played. We might have been different off the field but we had similar instincts about cricket. As a captain he had an attacking approach and I was at one with him – there was never an inclination to defend. He couldn't come to terms with defending a small total in the one-day game. He asked for no favours or declarations. And he was a hugely better bat than people gave him credit for. He would sacrifice himself in the interest of the team. If he'd been selfish he would have scored many more runs.'

This evaluation of Close by a master craftsman is not out of place here. Test selectors, members at Headingley and Taunton couldn't always make up their mind. Did he fully size up to the gutsy cult figure that his loyal fans claimed him to be? Did he antagonise players who fell short of his standards? Will future generations look back and heap the praise that has on occasions been too elusive? I am convinced that they will.

Cartwright himself was in no doubt. He warmed to a fellow rebel, one who bristled as he saw sham and duplicity through the various veneers in the committee rooms. Like Close, he was and remains an individualist, hating regimentation and hackneyed trends.

One inevitably comes back, in the case of Cartwright, to the mesmeric accuracy of his bowling. It isn't that we tend to ignore the kindly, esoteric skills of his coaching or the underrated proficiency of his batting. But, like Derek Shackleton, his precision never let him down. *Precision* is a favourite word of his; its importance was something he acquired and never forgot during his formative winter months on the assembly-line. He tells how, even blindfolded, he could land the ball on the same minute blade of grass. There is nothing boastful in the claim; indeed he cites others, like Glamorgan's Don Shepherd, who could also do it. Tom was a useful footballer and one imagines he was just as accurate, in matters of geometry, when it came to crossing the ball from the right wing.

A team-mate told me he felt singularly comfortable fielding short-leg for Cartwright. It was unthinkable that a delivery would be even marginally off course, to allow the suggestion of a liberty from the batsman. Whatever his critics implied, Tom used his fielders in attacking positions. As for his wicket-keeper, the bowler liked him to stand right up to the stumps. No one did this better, with intuitive vigilance, than Derek Taylor. They worked marvellously in tandem for Somerset. Cartwright possessed the perfect action. He hit the seam with a regularity. He went after wickets in an exercise that was as much cerebral as practical.

His parting from Somerset was probably the nadir of his career. Home life at tranquil Wells was fulfilling; the children were doing well locally at the Blue School. Joan, his wife, had no wish to move. But those unequivocal exchanges in the men's lavatories at the Weston-super-Mare cricket ground, his word not believed, were too rancorous ever to be undone. Cartwright, a proud and principled man, was so wounded that he threatened to sue the club. 'I didn't actually have a contract with Somerset. It was an agreement – I've always stood by my word.' And now his word, when it concerned his fitness to play cricket, was being questioned.

He went to Glamorgan, partly because Ossie Wheatley, with whom he'd played for Warwickshire, was the county chairman. Before deciding, he rang

Bernard Hedges, the Glamorgan professional who had been his best man. For Joan it meant going home; for Tom there were the prospects of a future beyond playing. He played indeed no more than seven times, apart from one day matches, for his third county, long enough though to take 4-46 against Yorkshire at Sophia Gardens. Retiring at the end of that 1977 season, he became Glamorgan's team manager before being appointed coaching officer to the Welsh Cricket Association and in turn the inaugural national coach.

Tom and Joan

Hundreds of schoolboy cricketers, some initially with scant regard for the game, came under his influence. He could be a social worker as well as a bowling instructor. His work wasn't always done when he walked away from the nets with his pupils. Not all by any means of his pupils ended up as county trialists but most of them were better cricketers than when they first came under this tutelage.

The composition of the Somerset and Glamorgan teams at various times reflected his excited eagle eye. While at Taunton one of his private missions was to find an outstanding black player. Brearley had recently returned from the West Indies and Cartwright asked him who might be emerging. Viv Richards' name was mentioned with some enthusiasm, and Rohan Kanhai confirmed it. Back at Taunton, Len Creed, the Bath bookmaker who had been out to Antigua, was also making his own claims for Richards who had already been brought back to this country by him. 'We've got to convince the committee,' Creed said to Cartwright.

'Well, bring him down to the ground.'

Richards, lean and shy, batted for 35 minutes. 'He didn't hit a ball off the square but it was perfect. Perfect. So still as he made his shot. I could have put a pint of beer on his head and he wouldn't have spilled a drop.'

Creed took the early risk and deservedly basked in the praise for his judgment that followed. We shouldn't exclude Cartwright entirely in the allocation of acclaim for Somerset's most sensational acquisition.

Throughout Cartwright's life, shafts of idealism have been discernible. There were the shopfloor politics in Coventry and much later, amid the unemployed and the silent pits of South Wales, uplifting talk for the human spirit at the side of an improvised net. His search for a black cricketer to inspire Somerset was perhaps another example of sub-conscious political realism.

It pleases him that he has come full circle, emotionally, in his association with Warwickshire. There, he started at £5 a week, novice eyes glistening and fruitful years away from his bruising departure. Much more recently, he has been back as president of the Old County Cricketers' Association.

He's a loyal man and Tiger Smith recurs in his conversations. 'He taught me so much about cricket and life. He showed me the value of the passing on of knowledge.'

Tom Cartwright pauses. 'Knowledge is for sharing, you know.' Once again his socialism isn't far away.

Reg Sinfield had a long, almost comic, chin of Jack Hulbert proportions, an avuncular face full of creases and crevices as well as good nature, and a boxer's battered nose. Perhaps we should deal with his pugilism first.

There was surely never a less bellicose man. For the whole of his sporting life he was surrounded by friends: players, umpires, neighbours, churchgoers. The voice, loyal as the Hertfordshire vowels he defiantly maintained, dissuaded others from any hints of enmity. Charlie Parker was his greatest friend in first-class cricket. And Charlie, pointedly patronised by the game's elders, and fatuously snubbed by successive Test selectors, was possessed of a combustible personality. It was Reg who finally led Parker away from the lift-cage at the Grand Hotel in Bristol in 1926 when he held Plum Warner menacingly by the lapels and offered a monologue of unequivocal invective at the expense of the Gloucestershire CCC's principal dinner guest whom he was convinced had for bigoted reasons curtailed his career. 'Come on, Charlie, it's not worth it,' said Sinfield, however much sympathy he and his fellow professionals had for the wonderful slow bowler with one Test to show for those bountiful Cotswold skills.

So why the boxer's nose? He was taught to step into a ring to defend himself, first in his years with CB Fry's training ship *Mercury* and then in his naval days at Devonport, Harwich and Scapa Flow. It was a rugged apprenticeship, part of an enforced ethos of physical courage and culture. Reg was strong and muscular; he was an obligatory contestant when it came to inter-service tournaments. He was encouraged to swing his youthful, artisan arms. Popularity was earned at a price; that over-exposed nose was to remain endearingly misshapen.

Reginald Albert Sinfield, Gloucestershire's first professional to complete the double and eye-blinkingly a Test cricketer in 1938, was among my true heroes. Yet he wasn't remotely a dashing batsman, laden with audacious strokes, capable of lighting up a drab day at Nevil Road. Indeed he was inclined to be one-paced, stubborn, even mechanical in the execution of his shots. He saw it as a duty, the sheer discipline drilled into him by Fry, to preserve his wicket. Taunting opponents around the boundary had no effect on him. Once in a barber's shop at Taunton, his face obscured by lather, he heard the occupants of adjoining chairs, blaspheming his obduracy at the county ground the previous day. "Bloody Sinfield. Talk about Bank Holiday cricket. Enough to drive us to sleep." He'd been playing under orders from his captain, Bev Lyon. Reg had the soap wiped from his shaven face, paid and escaped with suitable anonymity. He was not a cricketer fashioned for poets. He even antagonised the supporters of my native county of Somerset. Why then does he remain my favourite?

I suspect I am influenced by the sweetness of his nature. He died in 1988, aged 87, from bowel cancer. Up to a year or so before that he was climbing precariously up ladders to mend a neighbour's roof, mixing cement, tending his and others' gardens, motoring 32 miles a day in a clapped-out Morris 10, still to coach the boys at Colston's School. He doggedly defied his years like no-one else I can recall. His physical strength, contrasting with his innate gentility, was phenomenal.

A few days before he died, at the home of his step-son, Geoffrey and wife Ros just down the road from his own house in the village of Tickenham, near Clevedon in North Somerset, I paid one of several visits to his bedside. He was a religious man and he asked me to read some scriptural passages to him. I looked at him as I did so and he seemed restful, his eyes shut as if reflecting on the words. He had been both churchwarden and sidesman at the parish church, attending twice a Sunday and ready to let the vicar know how he disapproved if a sick villager had not been visited. But my call, that last time, was certainly not one of unrelieved piety.

'Come on, Reg, show me that grip again.'

A frail hand emerged from under the bedclothes. He grinned and, with an imaginary ball, showed me. 'All a matter of flight. Beat 'em in the air, boy.'

We were back on cricket – and the weary, watery eyes were sparkling again.

'Gloucestershire didn't want to give me my cap, you know, in 1926. They could be mean about that. Colonel Robinson, the captain, said I hadn't done enough to earn it. "Let's see what happens at Trent Bridge then, Colonel," I told him.'

Self-justification shouldn't really have been necessary. The single-minded intent was however almost ruined by Harold Larwood.

'He brought one back across my body and caught me in the worst possible place. I went down in a heap and got carted off. But back I came to complete my hundred. And Lol Larwood, bless his heart, later brought me in a double brandy.'

Nothing could have been more eloquent, in Sinfield's murmured argument for a cap. The Colonel handed one over. 'Should damn well think so,' said the team-mates in unison.

On that final visit of mine, he periodically closed his eyes and drifted away. I continued to chat about cricket and he would nod. Once or twice he opened his eyes to put me right on a point. Reg appropriately died in his grey cricket socks.

He was a player who never moaned, never showed dissent at a bad decision. Colleagues would see him looking skywards, suppressing an honest judgement, and they would chuckle. Umpires liked him because of this lack of brimstone. 'In 1936 at Bristol, against Hampshire, I saw Phil Mead coming in. I knew his weakness, needing to get off the mark with a tickle round to leg. So I asked Bev if I could have four short legs. He didn't think much of that but still agreed. Phil got quite confused and my first ball hit him on the pads, right in front. What did Tiger Smith do? He put his finger up – and said NOT out!'

Sinfield had a good memory like many ex-cricketers. One story about an umpire would lead to a warm-hearted cascade of them. 'Oh yes, against Middlesex at Lord's. I got on pretty well with Gubby but I don't know why he appealed – and successfully – against me for lbw. The ball hit the middle of my new Gunn & Moore bat and left a mark. You just accepted these things.

'They were balanced out, boy. I remember Frank Chester saying I was batting well enough to be on my way to a double. Then Jack Lee, the Somerset leg-break bowler, appealed for a catch behind. I even started walking. But Frank called me back and told me I'd missed it by six inches. I wasn't convinced ...'

Reg didn't tell jokes, yet his tales about his contemporaries hum with humour. Other counties used to claim that Gloucestershire in the pre-war and immediate post-war years were not the most cordial of opponents. Bill Andrews, renowned for his sweeping judgements – attributable to instinct rather than any element of malice – would say he could never understand why Gloucestershire looked so miserable. "I'd shout out Good Morning to them – and only dear old Reg Sinfield seemed to acknowledge."

Sinfield was generous in his morning greetings, as well as in giving encouragement to nervous, fallible county colleagues. Harry Smith, the Gloucestershire wicket keeper, was much liked and admired by Reg who could only recall his ever putting one catch down off his bowling. Vic Hopkins, from the village of Dumbleton, was brought in as a possible successor. But he was apt to get in a fearful state, keeping to Tom Goddard's off spinners in particular. He also dropped a few off Sinfield. 'Don't worry about it,' was the kindly response. Then Andy Wilson arrived from Lord's. His Gloucestershire debut was fraught with anxieties. He put down one catch and missed a stumping, and must have felt like heading straight back to Paddington and maybe pursuing that fledgling career as a Queens Park Rangers winger.

'Sorry, Mr Sinfield. Having difficulty picking up the flight.'

'Forget it, son. Come to the ground half an hour earlier tomorrow and we'll have a bit of a practice. Just the two of us.'

On the Hamble, in his *SS Mercury* days, amid the spartan conditions and the iron discipline that verged on sadism, Sinfield was seen by CB Fry as a useful cricketer. It made life a little easier for him. When he faltered in mathematics, he was told by Fry: 'Sinfield, instead of punishment, you can give me some batting practice. It was not unusual for the session to last for two hours. Fry demanded half volleys; Sinfield learnt the art of pitching on a spot. Accuracy remained one of his precious assets on the cricket field.

Reg, son of a Hertfordshire builder, was always consumed with the ethic of hard work and a sense of personal dignity. He accepted that in the process of character-building, life would not necessarily be easy. The unrelenting daily routine on *Mercury* was still a shattering experience to most of the boys. Years later, as Reg reflected more and more on those months as a boy sailor on the training ship, he confided to me how cruel and unnatural some of the discipline was. 'We were made to run along gravel paths in bare feet. Our feet didn't bleed because they'd become so hardened by then, but I think it was wrong.' Freudian and inhumane, I would say. Reg blamed Mrs Fry especially.

He went to *Mercury* at the age of 15, an unworldly village boy blessed with strong arms, a vague ambition to become a professional cricketer or soccer centre half, and typical of working class culture in those days, an unchallenging willingness to do what he was told. In 1916 he joined the Royal Navy.

After the war it was suggested there might be a living in county cricket for him. It must have helped when he played against an MCC side which included Jack Hearne, Nigel Haig, Patsy Hendren and FT Mann; he dominated the match in that sheepish way of his, by scoring 90 and taking six wickets. His father probably couldn't afford to employ him but by now the building trade held minimal appeal. An invitation came for him to join the groundstaff at Lord's. 'I wasn't shown much encouragement and was told I was unlikely to make the grade. Didn't fancy that, boy.' And soon he was gone.

Instead he joined Gloucestershire. It was hardly fair in his first county match in 1925, to come up against Fred Root, that crafty exponent of inswing. Sinfield sparred like a Hertfordshire novice, and was out twice without scoring. His background, again reinforced by Fry's philosophy, had instilled in him an inner resolve. Soon he was to battle for 83 against Glamorgan at Bristol.

Before long he was to prove himself one of county cricket's respected journeymen. He wouldn't have known how to play a flashy shot or give his bat an ostentatious twirl. He refused to shout in triumph when he took a wicket. Reg moved up the order, first to open with Alf Dipper. At this distance, the pairing seems devoid of imagination. They could both be dour fighters not adept at revising their approach. There wasn't too much style about their batting, yet they cussedly and efficiently frustrated a succession of fast bowlers. 'Come on, Reg, you and Dip must get a move on.' In fact, in their predominantly stodgy, conscientious manner, they did. The scoreboard, no doubt an improvised one on the out grounds, so often indicated that the slowcoach couple were scoring faster than they appeared to be.

After Dipper came Charlie Barnett. Here was a more logical combination. Reg could continue to be cautious, staying half the day if asked to, and Barnett, The Guv'nor, as the other pros called this ex-public schoolboy, went for his shots. Charlie was usually in a hurry, as if he wanted to knock off his hundred before lunch and then catch the end of the Berkeley Hunt, as the fox fringed his family's farmland.

And, of course, there was Wally Hammond to sustain the bravura. Reg shared some of the general reservations about Wally and his tendency to move away from the others socially. But the two got on well. When Hammond was gravely ill after his return from the West Indies tour of 1925-26, Sinfield was one of the few pros encouraged to visit him in the private nursing home in Clifton. 'I really thought he was a goner. Oh dear, he looked awful.'

Hammond knew that Gloucestershire had need of a grafter or two, like Sinfield. Sub-consciously he didn't want to see too many of his team-mates flashing a flamboyant blade. Charlie Dacre, the New Zealander who often irritated Hammond by his flurry of attacking shots and then untimely dismissal had too sacrificial an attitude for the great England batsman's liking. Sinfield was a reliable man for a crisis - and Gloucestershire, an ill-balanced team at times, had plenty of those before the war. He was also a genuine all-rounder, achieving the double for his county in 1934 and 1937. Those flighty off breaks remained a mystery to a surprising number of established batsmen. What would the Aussies make of him if he went on the 1936-37 tour?

'Listen to the wireless,' Hammond told him with some apparent authority. 'You're going to be in the party. Don't you believe me? I'll give you a fiver if you aren't.'

The inside knowledge was unreliable – and Hammond paid his debt. In addition, he showed loyalty to his West Country colleague. For the opening Test against Australia at Trent Bridge in 1938, Sinfield made his debut for his country. So did Bill Edrich and Doug Wright. By now an amateur, a transition that left some of his county team-mates in disbelief – though others claimed they had always expected as much because of his 'orchestrated sponsorship' by Plum Warner – Hammond led England for the first time.

There were seven centuries, two of them doubles, in a drawn match. Sinfield was down the order at number nine and was soon bamboozled by Bill O'Reilly. He took two wickets, the most prized being that of Bradman in the first innings. Les Ames had taken the catch, though he'd also appealed for a stumping to make absolutely sure. Arthur Wellard took over for the next Test, at Lord's. The call to Sinfield, in truth perhaps not quite a good enough bowler or batsman at the very highest level, never came again.

He was not a sportsman consumed with ambition to appear on a more illustrious stage. County cricket suited him, an honest day's sweat and then home to bed. He was a simple man, influenced by heart rather than intellect. The occasional headline of acclaim in the Bristol papers still pleased him, however, as did the way he would be asked for advice about the state of the wicket. 'Wally and Bev used to take me out to have a look at the pitch. Wally would say: "What do you think, Reginald?" Then he'd pause and say to Bev: "We need to know, don't we, because he's got to bowl the buggers out."

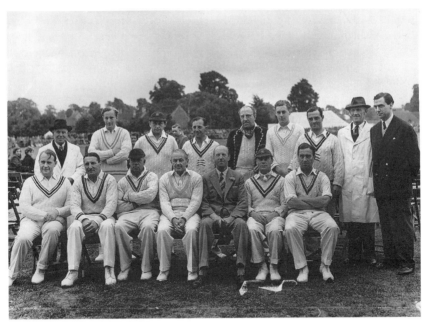

Sunday match at Badminton in aid of Andy Wilson's testimonial, 1953
Standing: unknown umpire, Ian Mitchell, Billy Griffith, Bill Edrich,
Bev Lyon, David Carpenter, Jack Young, Reg Sinfield, John Arlott
Sitting: Lord Cobham, Charles Barnett, Bob Wyatt, Gubby Allen,
Duke of Beaufort, Errol Holmes, Denis Compton

Reg played 423 matches for Gloucestershire between 1924-39 and scored 15,674 runs. Ten times he passed 1000 runs in a season; in all there were 16 hundreds, most of them painstakingly compiled, the best (209 not out) against Glamorgan in Cardiff. He batted for nearly eight hours, quite happy for Barnett to parade the adventure and front-foot aggression. It is easy, indeed understandable, for a sportsman to be affected by envy. Sinfield retained a genuine admiration for those he saw as more talented team-mates.

There were days, however, when Hammond, Barnett and the others accepted that he was best of all. It was certainly true when the South Africans came to Cheltenham in 1935. Gloucestershire had lost seven on the trot and were supposedly bereft of confidence. Dallas 'Puggy' Page, not so long out of Sandhurst and soon to die tragically in a road accident on the way home from the ground, was captain. It was always important to win the toss on the College ground and get runs on the board. 'Up to you, Reg. You know you like that short boundary down the slope.'

Sinfield, watched by the clerics, the ex-military and rows of schoolboys who had apparently delayed their holidays, was warmly cheered as he scored a century. He did intermittently turn and pull the ball down the shimmering slope. Just as well he did: Hammond was beaten by a googly to everyone's surprise when he was moving into the handsome mode which had suggested another of his big scores. He redeemed that lapse with a perfect hundred in the second innings. The South Africans were ultimately left to score 289. And for some time it appeared to be a perfunctory task.

Charlie Parker, Tom Goddard, Reg Sinfield

In truth they were all out for 201 – and it was down to Sinfield. He shifted any apportioning of praise to a ladybird. This was the first story about his career he ever told me, many years ago, and it illustrates the extent of superstition in sport. Some players even today insist on being the last out of the pavilion and onto the field; some would never strap on a left pad before a right one; bowlers can be seen rubbing their palms on the ground; batsmen, in the comic spirit of Philip Mead, go through extraordinary rituals after taking guard and before receiving the first ball. Reg's superstition was apparently more unusual.

He usually took his place in the spin bowler's queue behind Parker and Goddard. On that August day in 1935 he assumed that he would not be given a bowl at all. 'Then suddenly I saw a ladybird on my shirt. I went up to "Puggy" Page and said I thought it might be my lucky day. I asked if he'd let me have an over or two before lunch. He agreed and I quickly took two wickets.'

After the interval he was impatient to keep going. He had had nothing to eat and, when the game resumed, he was the opening bowler. He took three more wickets and Gloucestershire, against every prediction, had won. His analysis was 5-31. The South Africans were left bemused; they had failed to fathom those slightly odd off-breaks. Half an hour after the triumph, the crowd were reluctant to leave. The Mayor, civic chain jangling in excitement, made a special improvised speech. Page, his hair more neatly sleeked back than ever, said a few words – on the ground where once he had played as a sixth former. The spectators called for Wally and he waved in acknowledgement. 'And what about Reg?' someone shouted. He was not a natural hero, not the kind to win matches on his own. In team groups, he liked to be in the back row. 'They're calling for you, Reg,' said his team-mates. Reluctantly he half stepped forward and lifted a bronzed arm in response to the cheers.

That occasion symbolised Sinfield, the Cricketer. Wally, Tom and the two Charlies knew his self-effacing worth. There was something reassuringly constant about him.

At the crease he made shots that were never memorable and were yet laden with a village boy's common sense and resolve. He was a batsman who made more runs on the leg side. His concentration was prodigious. He had seen his father perspiring as he tried to make a decent living as a small-time builder. Reg believed there was something noble about sweating in hard work, either for a Stevenage employer or a cricket team.

As for his bowling, it simply couldn't be categorised with accuracy. 'Well, he was really a sort of off-spinner,' his colleagues would say, implying that he didn't quite conform. He was reliant on flight a good deal more than spin and would admit that he used to study the action and technique of Somerset's Jack White, whose considerable skills as a slow bowler had precious little to do with a turning ball. He also copied the deceptive manner with which 'Farmer' could hold one back. Reg bowled with his cap on. He nagged away at the off stump, an unfussy master of perfect length. But he was not afraid to experiment. His contemporaries argued that his most lethal delivery was a leg-cutter. Four times he took more than 100 wickets in a season. In 1936 his tally was 161; they included his 9-111 against Middlesex at Lord's. 'That particularly pleased me, boy,' he twinkled with a sly, though not unkindly, dig at cricket's headquarters where his emerging talents were inclined to be dismissed.

So he should not be viewed as bland. A grievance could probably be harboured. In his time as a senior pro in Bristol he was once asked his opinion of Dudley Pope when clearly the county did not want to retain him. 'He'll get a hundred for you one day, you've got to be patient.' They weren't and he joined Essex. In what poignantly was Pope's last first class match, he was playing against Gloucestershire and going well. 'I was the bowler and I made sure he completed his century.' That was at the Wagon Works ground in Gloucester. A few weeks later, Pope was another cricketer killed in a road accident.

Sinfield gave up playing in 1939. He had shown better form that year than in the previous one. Bev Lyon was still up to his plausible tricks, this time persuading the Oxford skipper to agree to a regenerated final day after the rain had seemed to ruin the match. Bev came out best in the calculations, of course, and Reg chuckled at the good-natured subterfuge. The two liked each other; Lyon had little time for social demarcation lines and was happier in the company of the pros in any case. That was why he liked to drive them in his Roller to what he quaintly called "my London pub". It was the Dorchester. It has to be said, all the same, in this cameo on the human condition, that while the pros loved Lyon and his democratic whims, they were still less than comfortable gulping their customary pints in the ambience of shaded lights and cocktail music on the piano.

Sinfield turned to coaching after the war. This was something he found he could do with paternal gentleness. He was at Clifton College for a quarter of a century, where his pupils included the towering, lean John Cleese, a budding off-spinner of sorts, one enraptured by the coach's ability to convey enthusiasm and technical knowledge. From Clifton, Reg moved to Colston's School in Bristol and his outstanding cricketing student was Chris Broad. 'You can play for England and be a second Frank Woolley,' he told the young left-hander.

Successive generations of young players came under his kindly influence. They privately marvelled that he was still such an active coach when in his mid-80s. As for his schools, they accepted that he saved them pounds by mending and restoring bats and pads which could so easily have been thrown away. There was a discernible sense of endless thrift about him, one that emanated from his humble roots. When he motored home after a day's work, he would switch off the engine to run his old car down Tickenham Hill for the last two or three miles. He also repaired the rust patches on the bodywork with putty.

But thrift should not be confused with meanness. He had no children of his own – both wives predeceased him – but he put two step-sons through Millfield. At home, he had erected a net for family cricket practice.

He had as many theories about gardening as slow bowling. This was especially true of his tomato growing. "Reggie's veggies" was a standing family joke. He was proud of his plums and greengages, the saplings of which he had brought from his native parish of Benington, just outside Stevenage. He rarely arrived at the home of his step-son and his wife without fruits and vegetables, or barley sugars for their young daughter. I should hate to give the impression that Reg was insufferably saintly but, in the truest sense, he was a good man. Too many said so for that kind of evaluation to be ignored. 'He was an upholder of all the basic things that mattered – truth, honesty, and loyalty. In his homely way he was a person of great integrity,' a villager told me some years after Reg had died.

At the time of his death he was England's oldest surviving Test cricketer. He was already 37 for that cherished, if solitary, appearance. In his later life he needed no excuses to reminisce: mostly about his fellow players and hardly ever about himself. There was for him more conversational mileage in Gloucestershire's match with the Australians in 1930. It was laden with memories, not least because it ended in a tie. Lyon, flushed with post-match excitement, ordered an extra big gin-and-tonic and told everyone within hearing: 'Anybody can win or lose the game – not many can manage a bloody tie. Certainly not against the Aussies.' Sinfield, at a time when he could still bowl at medium-pace, had taken the new ball with Barnett before leaving affairs to Parker and Goddard. He also opened the batting. 'Not a great game for me, boy. But I did bowl Bill Ponsford and got Alan Kippax leg-before. What a match that was. Queues for miles outside the Fry's ground in Bristol. The gates had to be closed, you know. It was young Don Bradman, boy. Just made 200 odd in the Oval Test, he had ...'

He loved cricket yet there was always for this self-reliant fellow a life beyond the boundary. He was just as happy balancing with the unconcern of a steeplejack to replace a neighbour's tiles; or winning a prize in the village flower show with his tomatoes; or feeding his goldfish with porridge; or mending schoolboys' pads in his own time. Yes, Reg was an exceptional bloke.

JACK 'KID' BERG
(JUDAH BERGMAN)

1909 - 1991

Boxing champion and generous restaurateur.

I retain scant affection for boxing as a sport: not so for the boxers. The apparent dichotomy perplexes some of my friends and intimate members of my family. When once I returned from a regional boxing tournament, where I had been phoning graphic though mostly unqualified accounts of succeeding bouts to a local morning paper, my wife spotted blood on my shirt. The red corpuscles from an insensitively rearranged nose had sprayed the ringside press table. How, I was sternly asked back in the civilised haven of home, did I reconcile an evening watching such a crude and dangerous entertainment with those familiar self-righteous utterances of mine that anything as primeval as boxing, involving as it did calculated blows to the head, should be unequivocally indicted?

My ambivalence is not something I can easily explain. During the Sixties, my wife and I were invited to join the audience for a television programme in Cardiff, where that literate and loquacious Welshman Gwyn Thomas conversed with selected guests, most of whom had emotional links with the Principality. I went with some eagerness because Tommy Farr was among those appearing. He was articulate and relaxed under the strong TV lights. After the show, to Anne's surprise and no doubt embarrassment, I queued more than half an hour for the former boxer's autograph. When I had still been a small boy, hadn't my father tapped me gently on the shoulder before we'd tip-toed downstairs, not long before dawn, to sit in rapt awe in front of the cumbersome old wireless perched on the kitchen table, while Farr fought Joe Louis at Madison Square Garden?

In those days I knew little of the physical danger when two heavyweights attempted to belt each other into submission. To me it was immeasurable excitement and an indefinable glamour, emanating from the other side of the Atlantic. More than sixty years later I can still vividly picture that rare filial and parental bonding as we drank our cocoa in silence - and I prayed with the whole of Tonypandy, that Farr would win.

Boxers continued to stir my youthful imagination, not always by any means for their feats in the ring. I regarded Jack Doyle as much for his singing as his ringcraft (a reasonable judgment, as it turned out); I admired the way Larry Gains made his gentle racial statement and rode to hounds; I told myself that Eric (Boy) Boon, a blacksmith's son, was just as happy shoeing horses as parading his promise at the National Sporting Club (I was thrown into confusion when he started an acting career). I liked boxers for the wrong reasons: Peter Kane, the flyweight champion, because he had saucer eyes like Eddie Cantor, Jack Petersen, the intelligent Welsh heavyweight, because someone assured me, perhaps erroneously, that he was giving up boxing to become a doctor.

Early in the war Jock McAvoy came to my village to give a boxing exhibition for the Servicemen stationed in the area. What I remember was the sheer power of his punching, even in a makeshift ring under the beeches. Never before had I been in the presence of a professional boxer. I was not conscious that the ex-champion might be holding back. Instead I winced every time his gloves sank into his sparring partner's fleshy midriff. Mercifully it lasted for only three rounds and then the two slung their uniforms over their shoulders and wandered off together, lighting a cigarette as they went. That kind of post-fight sentimentality always fascinated me.

Just after the war I took my first ingenuous steps as a journalist. South Somerset was hardly renowned for professional boxing; it was all the more startling then when our senior sports reporter found himself being subpoenaed for a libel action, brought by two local promoters against *The People* for suggesting the bill might not have been quite what it claimed to be. In the years that followed I was to discover how often the public might be short-changed. Could there be another sport in which impressionable spectators see something that varies so consistently from the published promises? And that doesn't take into account all those risible mis-matches.

When I was a 17-year-old, desperate to augment my 25 shilling a week wages as a copy-boy, a rumour reached the reporters' room that an improvised gym had been erected at the rear of the Coronation Hotel in the town and that a brilliant American boxer was being secretly trained. It was not a pub any of us, however thirsty in our self-conscious apprentice days, patronised. But I went to see the landlord, who rather grandly confided that he had a future world middleweight champion on his hands and that, well, a line or two of well constructed publicity would not be inappropriate.

I spoke to the boxer, an unsophisticated, amiable young man and then, rather daringly, sent 500 words to *Sporting Record*, which fortuitously for me was trying to make some modest inroads with its West Country circulation. I knew nothing at all about big-time boxing or the manner the fight game was structured. As a potential national sports writer I was so naïve that I sent my piece in long-hand. It was a glowing vignette of a 23-year-old hillbilly boxer making spectacular progress in this country and only one stage removed from a title fight. By return I received a letter of extravagant appreciation from Graham Selkirk, who I believe was then the editor of *Sporting Record*. 'We like your piece and shall be using it. You will receive 7/6d by the end of the month. And we should like to receive regular contributions about the West Country from you.'

For the next 12 months my wages were blissfully augmented. Alas, my hillbilly hero went rapidly into obscurity in the process. The next time I walked into the Coronation, the gym had disappeared.

So who instead became my boxing hero? In 1951 I was doing my National Service in the RAF and was stationed for several months at Colindale in London. Most nights I would go down the Northern Line to the West End, to pick up free theatre seats or watch try-out music hall acts at the Nuffield Centre, just off Charing Cross station; or occasionally to prowl, in the wide-eyed ways of country boys, the back alleys of Soho. One evening, I was strolling aimlessly round the corner from Jack Solomons' gym in Great

Windmill Street when I saw a man standing in the doorway of his restaurant. He was small, and resplendent in a tuxedo.

I was in uniform, an obligatory form of patriotic identification if I needed seats at the Nuffield Centre. And it was clearly the uniform that attracted his attention.

"Where are you stationed, then?"

I was already well versed in the smarmy invitations from clipjoint operators, pimps and con-men. This was a different kind of conversation. It went on for ten minutes, during which time he told me he'd also been in the RAF. 'Feel like something to eat?'

I gave the sort of helpless shrug that implied a young National Serviceman was really in no position, financially, to go into a Soho restaurant. 'No,' he said, sensing my unease, 'on the house. It isn't very busy tonight.'

In truth it wasn't busy at all. I was the only customer - and I was about to be paid for. He brought me a steak and waved aside my offer to make at least some kind of contribution. While he had been gone - I suspect business may have been so bad that he was the chef as well - I noticed for the first time a number of boxing stills on the walls. I went to examine them: they all featured the same man, the dapper figure who had asked me in for a free meal. Jack 'Kid' Berg.

3, DENMAN STREET,
W.1

PHONE:
GERRARD 8700

JOLSON'S
RESTAURANT & DELICATESSEN BAR

PROPRIETORS: JACK (KID) BERG AND
FAY ROSENBLUM

We talked boxing for a long time after that, or rather he talked. He didn't patronise me in my ignorance. Nor did he boast of his conquests or the acclaim that his flamboyant presence once engendered. At the same time he had a sang-froid about him that I envied. My deferential attitude was probably excessive; village boys aren't very adept at disguising idolatry. When I left, I thanked him profusely and never saw him again. Soon, I was to read he had deserted the restaurant business and was going into films, not for the first time, but now as a stunt man. How he must have hated the sheer inactivity of standing in the doorway of a relatively deserted restaurant. Kid Berg was never a stationary man. He had chased around the East End streets, keeping just out of trouble, as a pallid child. He had been perpetual motion in every ring he entered. On his many voyages to the States he had played games on deck or danced till dawn in the ship's ballroom. When once before the war he was given the lead in a feature film, he'd cockily told the director: 'I hope there's plenty of action.'

I came late to his fighting style: after the rump steak, in fact. I began reading insatiably about him. One can see why the Americans liked him so much. He knew one single, pragmatic way to fight and that was by going forward. He possessed an enormous reservoir of energy. There were times in his early career when he boxed twice a week. He was unfailingly exciting, lifting spectators out of their seats. His methods rarely came from the boxing manual yet the ringcraft could be quite bewildering. His combination of punches staggered opponents steeped in orthodoxy.

Much of his money was made in the States. He became the world junior welterweight champion. Most bouts involving him were memorable. The American promoters struggled to find opponents who had a genuine chance of offsetting his inimitable bravura. Ancient wiseacres out there still talk of his great fights with Kid Chocolate, the talented Cuban Negro, and Tony Canzoneri. In 1930 and '31 he defended his title nine times in America. He was the British lightweight champion at his first attempt in 1934. Such dour historical statistics I can recite - but they tell nothing of his piston fists or gambolling feet snatched straight from an up-tempo Charleston.

His handlers simply glanced at each other and wondered aloud whether he would burn himself out. When he had a bad fight, there was talk of retirement. Those sentiments seldom came from Berg. He enjoyed it too much; he liked making money; he was an easy going extrovert - not so easy going in the ring - who embraced the glamour, the headlines, the publicity and the parties. His first wife Bunty was a dancer in the chorus line with Anna Neagle - and C.B. Cochrane was the best man at the wedding. He used to ride down Rotten Row in Hyde Park on Sunday mornings. His blonde second wife, Morya, had been a beautician. He always demanded a good-looking young woman on his arm.

The East End threw up some gifted Jewish boxers. Ted 'Kid' Lewis is one cherished name. There was also Harry Mizler, known at Hymie, who surrendered his lightweight title to Berg. The build-up to that fight hadn't been entirely edifying. Here were two Jewish boys of different styles, with their own noisy coteries of East End supporters. There was much talk of grudge and even Jewish monopoly. The ugly aspects of Mosley were starting to emerge too; anti-Semitic emotions were strong in bigoted corners of which there were many.

As the fight approached, Berg was winning the battle of column-inches. He knew how to manipulate the press. He was an altogether more colourful character than Mizler whose family had a fish stall just off the Commercial Road. There was an uneasy tension that preceded the title bout; it never went away and was climaxed when both boxers ended up sharing the same dressing room, neither prepared to concede ground and move out. As controversies were compounded, the wily old Harry Levene was left rubbing his hands.

The Mizler towel was thrown in at the end of the eighth round. There was, I recall, a print of that strange, anti-climactic scrap on the wall of the Berg's restaurant. Both boxers had the

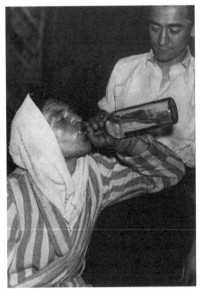

Training in the 1930s

Star of David emblazoned on their shorts. Berg had badly wanted that fight and asked Levene to obtain it. The Berg-Mizler contest was to me so much more than a boxing match for a title. It was a piece of enthralling social and political history. Judah Bergman's (Kid Berg's) parents were Russian-Jewish. In the early years of the century, the claustrophobic back streets of the East End reverberated with Hebrew cadences. The refugees were starting life afresh. They might have had a sense of relief from racial oppression but they knew there was a minimal guarantee of work. They were defensive and sensitive, quick-tempered and quick-witted. Their business initiative, at even the most humble level, was envied by their Gentile neighbours. They were warm-hearted and sentimental, especially among their own. The ghetto mentality was inevitable but gradually their single minded skills grew - as tailors, stallholders, kosher cooks ... and boxers.

Kid Berg had learned how to defend himself in the mean Whitechapel streets with his restless, flailing arms and fists. He had also learned from his parents how to look after his pennies. It was an ethnic art he never lost, despite the showy lifestyle that he embraced and the moments of generosity as pretty blondes fluttered their eyelids. He didn't need too many advisors as he kept fighting and the cheques came in. He successfully dabbled in property for a time. When he moved from his first wife to his second, he opportunistically used the same ring.

He was the Whitechapel Whirlwind in a fight game bedecked with melodramatic fancy names. Mostly he was known simply as Yiddle. It carried affection for the man, not a prejudicial sneer for his race. 'Come on, Yiddle,' the crowds bellowed. He responded with a bellicose ferocity that contrasted so sharply with the congenial demeanour of the dandy out of the ring.

Such paradoxes are part of the appeal of boxing that refuses to leave me, despite my nagging misgivings. I hate the mean-spirited vulgarity of the sport, with raucous morons screaming their obscenities from some of the best seats. I hate the sadists who want only to see gushing blood rather than deft instances of self-defence and other manifestations of the noble art. I hate the exploiters who historically have always bedevilled boxing. Some of the game's greatest practitioners have died penniless; not many promoters have.

During the late 80s I edited a book, *Hungry Fighters of the West*, which said rather more about the region in the ghastly days of the Depression than about those who boxed for a fiver a night. The publication, which quickly sold out, was my idea; I felt it would tell future generations more about Bristol's social history, of deprivation and abject poverty in the years between the wars, than many weighty academic tomes. Dozens of working class lads, their concave bellies distorted by lack of food, dreamt of being successful boxers. It was for almost all of them an inaccessible ambition.

There were regular boxing bills, staged in backstreet halls, converted swimming baths and minuscule cinemas, even erstwhile cowsheds in some of the surrounding villages. The atmosphere was heavy with smoke, Medical supervision was often no more than nominal. The wan young scrappers could frequently not afford a dressing gown or proper shorts. I talked much more recently to many of them, and one told me how he would fight three times in a day to bolster his earnings. It became evident that, apart from a few extra bob to augment the family meal table, they were also grasping - although unable to articulate the psychological process - for a transitory evening of glamour, however phoney, to elevate their spirits and mundane, meaningless lives.

Without exception the West Country boxers I chatted to had a gruff, honest charm. They remembered their supporting bouts in touching detail: the number of rounds they went, the number of bemused tumbles they took, the amount of the purse they placed into their back pockets. Then, in their bedraggled clothes again, they would walk with an air of acquired nobility and fleeting stature out of the fuggy hall, slapped on the bony back as if they were as big and impregnable as Bombardier Billy Wells, by their doting mates.

Kid Berg in the R.A.F.

Yet here, in Bristol, one of them, Jimmy Cooper, still a week short of his 15th birthday, died in the ring. He went down in the second round and never got up again. It was his sixth 'professional' fight. And the hall had not been licensed for boxing. Thousands lined the route for the funeral; those who wept at the graveside included his trainer and his young opponent. A city closed its shops for a time in respect of Jimmy Cooper. How could one possibly ignore such social history, such human drama, such communal love?

These disquieting episodes gnaw away at me, compounding my guilt over my sneaky peeps at a sport which still stirs my baser instincts and pulls me back for a squint through the keyhole. One thinks of Steve Watt, Young Ali, Johnny Owen and Joseph Sticklen who all died over recent years as the result of a boxing match. Those names come uncomfortably into my consciousness. No doubt there were others. Some like Michael Watson and, of course, Muhammad Ali, continue to suffer. How do we calculate the mental hazards? To what extent was boxing the cause of the suicides of Freddie Mills, Ben Foord and Randolph Turpin?

I return, however, to Jack Berg, the Yiddle, the pride of Whitechapel and Stepney. His faculties were unimpaired in old age. The fine head of hair, parted with sleek care in the middle, had by then given way to white curly wisps to match a broad, neatly trimmed moustache. He went along to the big fights, talked more rationally than most about the way the sport was going and kept his more cynical thoughts for intimate friends and his family. He carried a few scars and outward signs of bruising battles but not many. He was proud of them, his figurative scrapbook of triumphant fights, his Equity card and his appearance on *This is Your Life*.

It may be odd to opt for a hero, an imperishable one, that I met for less than an hour. Never have I enjoyed a rump steak more.

Kid Berg, with Tommy Farr, 1984

Blinkered though I may be by the emotional tug of geographical partisanship, it would surely still be difficult to name entries of heroic proportions to first-class cricket that could remotely equal those of two Somerset players, Harold Gimblett and Maurice Tremlett. The romantic minutiae of Gimblett's hundred at Frome in 1935, after he'd missed the country bus on the way to the ground, has been retold by successive generations of West Country schoolchildren. Reflections on Tremlett's ingenuous deeds are, as a subject for renewed wonderment, overdue.

His stage was Lord's, in the May of 1947, just as it began to shimmer and regain its hauteur after the war. He was not long out of the army and, inclined to be introvert by nature, was slightly overwhelmed by the whole idea of becoming a county cricketer and now actually invited by Somerset's canny old chancer of a captain, RJO Meyer, to make his debut at the game's hallowed headquarters.

Tremlett was well-built and blond, someone who stood out, an effect he never tried to cultivate. He walked with big strides and a movement that was apt to appear a little stiff-jointed, as if he were wandering along a side street in Taunton on market day rather than shaping like a 23-year-old recently in khaki. On reflection, half the Somerset side in those immediate post-war years seemed stiff in the joints. Arthur Wellard and Frank Lee had aged. Bertie Buse had a posture at the crease that was made for the cartoonists. Wally Luckes had his permanent constipation and Jack Meyer his lumbago.

Horace Hazell, Arthur Wellard, Maurice Tremlett,
Eric Hill, Bertie Buse, Frank Lee, Bill Andrews

116

For that match against Middlesex, no-one expected Somerset to win. No-one ever did. Test selectors chose not to explore talents across the Mendips and Quantocks. Somerset had finished fourth in the championship table the previous summer but surely that was a mistake: artificial matches and too much evidence that county cricket needed time to re-establish itself. Meyer had seen Tremlett in some Services matches and thought he should concentrate on his batting, even forget about his bowling. All the same he put him at number ten in the order, below another debutant, Eric Hill, and Luckes. Only Horace Hazell was below him. Horace bowled slow left-arm of unwavering accuracy: there were times when his greater value was as a dressing room joker.

Like Tremlett, Hill, tall, lean and correct, not long out of a Mosquito and brave photo-recce sorties, didn't really know what to expect in county cricket. In one of his earliest innings, he was at the wicket when Hazell waddled in. The umpires knew something of the newcomer's demeanour as a batsman.

'What are you going to have, Horace?' he was asked as he painstakingly took guard.

'Let's see, now – what have you got?'

Hill, a serious young man, still an amateur but hoping to become a professional to justify all the hours he had watched the county during his holidays from Taunton School, years later recalled 'Nutty' Hazell's brewery-weaned phraseology to the umpire and said: 'I had to ask myself what this game, at championship level, was all about.'

Somerset beat Middlesex by one wicket – and such a bald sentence tells us nothing. The cricket correspondent on *The Times* was altogether more extravagant. The narrow victory was achieved:

> ... after as noble a game of cricket as any man could ever hope to play in or any spectator be privileged to watch. Test matches may come and go, but a county match with a finish so tense and yet so friendly can in enjoyment never be excelled ... What fun it was, and what a pity that the ground was not packed to watch so grand a game.

This should go down in the cricket annals as Tremlett's Match. The newcomer took eight wickets in the game including a 5-8 spell in five overs. Everyone liked that pure, natural high action. He was above medium-pace, at times well above. He bowled straight and wasted little. He hit the deck hard and found some bounce. It wasn't so much the signs of movement; it was the endeavour, the challenge, the suggestion that there was so much to build on and natural pace to be refined. If he was nervous, at Lord's, it didn't show. In the Long Room, Gubby Allen was telling friends: 'I captained him, you know, when he was in the army. I told him he should come and join us at Middlesex.'

That was his bowling. But in the end he won the match with his batting: to earn considerable acclaim from the spectators and approval from Meyer. 'I told you that you could bat. Didn't know how well you could bowl, as well. You'll play for England if you carry on like this.'

Middlesex had gained a lead of 97 on first innings when Bill Edrich had scored a century. Then, as Tremlett took five wickets, they were all out for 78. Somerset needed 176 and, despite some middle-order resistance from the gritty Luckes and Hill, the game was slipping away from them. Both were out and Tremlett, with Hazell at the other end, numbers ten and eleven, were aware that they were still 15 runs behind at lunch. Temperament was not a worry; just once, Tremlett swung wildly at Young and was grateful to miss. Then, with perfect co-ordination he hit the slow bowler over long-off for six. The game was soon won with an on-drive.

As he and the little, beaming Hazell came in, the Middlesex players lined up to applaud them. It was a spontaneous gesture of congratulations, intended especially for the all-rounder most of them had never previously heard of.

It was a marvellous debut. Yet, as in the case of Gimblett, it brought a surfeit of premature acclamation. Neither of them really enjoyed it; they knew in their hearts it might not be sustained. Tremlett was immediately likened to Maurice Tate. Other misplaced comparisons were bandied about. The memories of that ill-judged tour of Australia only months earlier were still fresh in the mind. A nation was rashly told that Tremlett had a Test future.

At Alf Gover's, 1947

So he had. Gubby was constant in his praise. Others of relative eminence took a look. One or two even came across the Mendips. And Tremlett was named for the West Indies tour of 1947-48, as well as for South Africa the following winter. In total he played in three Tests, taking four wickets and scoring 20 runs. Those of us who had thrilled to his bowling and instinctive straight drives knew that something had gone wrong. Before he sailed for the Caribbean, he had been sent for two weeks to Alf Gover's indoor school in London. Did the tuition improve or only confuse him? Was he able, an uncomplicated player with natural talents, to absorb advice about technical adjustments?

Out in the West Indies, Allen and others encouraged him to lengthen his run-up and aim for additional speed. That was his undoing. Against Jamaica, he dismissed Frank Worrell; he came up with some bouncy deliveries and penetrative break-backs. But he was beginning to worry, too. 'Tremmy' was always a worrier.

Back at Taunton, some of that earlier zest, as he came up off that easy, controlled run, was missing. He was happy to be under-bowled. He talked more and more about concentrating on his batting. The narrative of his bowling decline is a sad one. It isn't completely unknown in the history of first-class cricket. The harder he tried to bowl a line, the more wayward his overs became. There were matches when the wides mounted alarmingly and his bronzed face was etched in turmoil.

Bill Andrews had given up playing and was coach at various times when Tremlett was there. His relationship with Maurice could be a trifle wary but he knew plenty about fast bowling and its technical demands. Bill said:

> Experience taught me never to try to change a bowler. Take the case of Maurice. He had me beat when he came back from the West Indies and South Africa. He came to Somerset as a natural bowler with a shortish run and a lovely action. After those two tours, he returned to county cricket unsure of his run-up. His beautiful rhythm and action seemed to have gone and his direction was all over the place. It was evident what had happened on those tours. Here was a challenge for me. I thought it was a chance to prove I was a good coach. But I failed completely. His arms were not working together and I considered this was due to a lack of confidence in his run-up.

Andrews was the good-hearted, controversial extrovert who dominated Somerset folklore before and after the last war. I mentioned that suggestion of unease with Tremlett, the bowler who in effect took over from Bill in the county team after that stirring arrival at Lord's.

When in 1956 Tremlett was appointed Somerset's first professional skipper (of which more later), Andrews was the coach. Significantly he wrote in his autobiography, *The Hand That Bowled Bradman*, a book he kindly asked me to edit: "He was a sound tactician. When a professional captain is appointed, things are generally made awkward for the coach. The captain is really the boss."

In those last few seasons before he gave up bowling altogether, many of us in the West Country, in the press boxes as well as around the boundary, shared Tremlett's visible agony. It angered us when insensitive souls loudly mocked his painful overs. I remember him once at Bath looking in the direction of his detractors. His expression, devoid of contempt or indeed self-pity, was saying: 'Try to understand what I'm going through – it won't be many more overs.' Nor was it. He continued to score runs attractively, without the lurking hints of neurosis that his uncoordinated bowling brought him.

Maurice Tremlett hitting a straight six at Taunton, 1957
The non-striker is Colin McCool

It was his batting that I first warmed to. He could loft a straight drive as well as anyone in the game. Opposing captains would see his long-striding approach to the crease and immediately station a long-on and long-off. He hit cleanly and straight, happiest when going for his runs. Back in the days of the London indoor school, Andy Sandham had stressed how keen Tremlett was to learn, while sounding a warning that it might not be easy to cure him entirely of a few bad technical habits. There were 16 hundreds, all the same, and he passed 1000 runs in a season ten times. On occasions the concentration would lapse, as if he were suddenly bored by the inevitable patterns of the match and he'd like to get back to the pavilion and act on Wellard's advice for the 3.30 at Wolverhampton. What everyone in the team liked about a player who could turn a game was his modesty. Playing against Gloucestershire in Bristol, he'd gone to Temple Meads station at the close of play to collect his wife, Lee, and take her by bus to Horace Hazell's home on the Brislington edge of the city.

She was always eager to know how he had got on. Lee had been a swimmer, a Western Counties' junior champion with Olympics potential and little interest in cricket before she met him. 'How d'you do today, Maurice?'

He offered no more than a non-committal shrug. 'OK'. And he changed the subject. He hardly ever brought his cricket home with him. They couldn't afford a car then and, as the bus rattled on its way to Brislington, Lee took a sideways glance at another passenger's evening paper. The back page headlines screamed out in regional delight: GREAT HUNDRED FOR TREMLETT.

Although born at Stockport and later to live briefly at Leamington Spa and Exeter – his father worked for the Post Office – Maurice was the archetypal Somerset cricketer. He was fallible with his bold shots; he liked to overwork the scoreboard operator; there was, at least for the most part, sunshine in the way he played. He wasn't too much bothered about reputations within the opposition: and he wasn't too much bothered about his average. He was an easy-going team man. The crowd responded to that.

In the late 40s and early 50s, Somerset were hardly the most proficient county side in the championship. They were, however, among the most convivial. There was a real community feel in the dressing room. Some of them had come back from the war with understandable strains of cynicism which they were inclined to direct at those they saw as the amateurs in the committee room. But away from the ground and the game's politics, the volume of fellowship was exceptional and heart-warming. At the close of play they would wander down, past the market, to the Crown and Sceptre, then renowned as the cricketers' pub. They drank strong pints and exchanged good-natured stories. Dutifully, well almost, they bought their rounds. Bertie Buse, it was claimed, would close his eyes and affect to snooze. His impeccable timing was unmasked by Tremlett. He winked at the others and asked in the quietest of voices: 'What are you going to have, Bert?'

The former solicitor's clerk was immediately wide awake. 'Double Diamond, Tremmy.'

Buse was a fine all-rounder. His benefit may have been a one-day disaster and for some reason he objected to John Arlott likening his quaint physical movements on the field to a butler dispensing the drinks. But in his slightly punctilious manner he was still much liked by the others. They all got on famously. Wellard, with whom Tremlett shared a room on away matches in the early days, had a healthy thirst. He taught Maurice out-swing and a few of the secrets of the race-track. Arthur would sometimes chase away after play to an evening race meeting or, at Bristol, an hour or two at the dogs. Sometimes he took Tremlett with him. Wellard was everyone's favourite: that of the West Country spectators because of the sixes he put into allotment plots and back gardens, that of his team-mates because of the racing tips he liberally passed on. Andrews, his mate, reckoned that Arthur could memorise every card in a pack. That may have been a marginal exaggeration; not so the fact that he liked to take out his false teeth in the hot weather, when fielding at silly mid-off, "to distract the batsmen".

Tremlett loved that. Wellard was the godfather to daughter, Julie, whose birth had been at the home of Hazell and his wife. That was the extent of the dressing room rapport. Johnny Lawrence, the little leg-spinner, often watched and tut-tutted. He was a devout Methodist who didn't exactly approve of all the drinking that went on – or the colourful language. Yet his strictures were offered with a tolerant Yorkshireman's half-smile as if God was prepared to overlook the occasional noggin. It wasn't just the players; the wives got on equally well together.

In the spirit of the times, though markedly less so than in the 20s and 30s, the professionals kept their own company. You wouldn't find Bunty Longrigg at the Crown and Sceptre or the richly talented Micky Walford, say, joining in a Hazell-inspired chorus or two. On train journeys, however, the Bath schoolmaster Fred Castle would pull the playing cards from his pocket and demonstrate his deserved membership of the Magic Circle.

That was the jolly side of cricket. But not everything was as affable, of course. Somerset were soon running out of captains. Some members of the committee and officials pretended that times and mores weren't changing. They continued to talk in the redundant phraseology of imperialist Britain. Murmurs that they might have at some point to contemplate a professional skipper brought reactions of horror. So they frantically looked for short-term solutions: decent backgrounds, nice voices and, well, reasonable cricketing knowledge. In 1948 Somerset had three official captains, doing the job in rotation and two of them on leave from the Sudan Political Service. It may have been only three in the official records; some of us counted at least five in transitory charge.

The 1955 captain was Gerry Tordoff, a Cambridge blue who somehow gained temporary release from the Navy. For a fourth season, Somerset ended on the bottom of the table. The finances were in disarray and morale was low. Tordoff's inexperience had been quickly exposed; he lasted for only one summer.

Tremlett's appointment, we can assume, was almost by default. Bristling, bigoted members of the committee trotted out the facile arguments. He lacked authority, too evidently one of the boys. Where was the evidence of leadership? How would this seemingly lackadaisical Tauntonian, who liked to place a bet and quaff a sociable pint, shake up a team of indeterminate, disparate talents?

In fact, the whispering campaign, among officials and senior committee, never disappeared. A few of them appeared to be bracing themselves to denounce him for any kind of weakness or misdemeanour. Their chance came after one disciplinary lapse among several players in Swansea. There was talk of sacking him, Harold Stephenson and one or two others. Tremlett, a popular figure within the team, survived that internal kerfuffle. The undeniable fact was that he was proving himself, in the tactical sense, a very good captain.

There were times when his case would have been improved with a more assertive personality. He might also have tried to develop a more productive communication with the committee. He consciously kept his distance; the mutual unease was nearly tangible on occasions. 'I've got little in common with them,' he'd say. 'They never wanted me as captain and they can't wait to get rid of me.'

That was possibly true, even though he had a number of loyal friends at the sub-committee meetings that were frequently called and at which his name was often high on the agenda. His critics saw him, although not by nature verbose or a trouble-maker, as basically anti-Establishment. They had discovered, too, that when in 1953 three local journalists dared to express a vote of no confidence in the way the county club was being run, leading to public meetings, much bad blood and duplicity on the part of those who represented the bewhiskered Somerset club, Tremlett was surreptitiously helping the journalists - Ron Roberts, Bob Moore and Eric Hill – with their administration, as the midnight oil was burnt.

'We must find another chap, socially right, you know, to succeed Tremlett,' the committee agreed. And, with a strange, wayward logic, they plumped for Squadron Leader Alexander (Alan) Shirreff. Dulwich, Cambridge blue, county cricket for Hampshire and Kent, and impressive statistics for Combined Services added up to a reassuring sum total of nicely rounded achievement. He was appointed as assistant secretary by Somerset, an unsubtle holding operation (which was anything but) as he waited for Tremlett to be demoted. This didn't happen and he left after one season, during which he fleetingly and bizarrely assumed the position of coach – at Andrews' expense. Bill was fired four times in all; he must have been immune from shock.

On the circuit, where opinions could be cutting, opposing skippers had a respect for Tremlett. They discovered that he retained a sort of card-index memory of players' strengths and weaknesses. Like that rumbustious old digger, Sammy Woods, a previous Somerset captain, Tremlett hated drawn games. He attempted to keep the other side interested on the last day when any chance of a result seemed to be drifting away.

Maurice Tremlett with George Emmett at Bristol, 1958

In 1958 he led Somerset to third in the championship table. Compliments, numerous and generous, came his way. They only irritated his critics who had cussedly refused to compromise their views about his so-called unsuitability. He had wonderful, wizened players like the Aussie pair, Colin McCool and Bill Alley, around him. The pipe-smoking McCool, who could be wise and withering at the same time, admired Tremlett and approved of the manner in which the captain remained pointedly taciturn in the company of the club officers and fusspot committeemen. There was Peter Wight, too, playing the sweetest of shots on the up – and Brian Langford often spinning the ball as well as anyone in the country, without a sniff of Test recognition.

I talked to Tremlett's wife, his son, Tim, and former team-mates. They all emphasised how much he loathed the cricket politics that dogged him during his years as county captain. Not once did he discuss them at home. But to those close to him on the field, the effect of the sniping could not be wholly disguised. His enthusiasm waned. There was even an occasion or two when he chose to wander off the third man boundary. 'Take over for a bit, Steve,' he asked a surprised Stephenson.

He'd had enough. All his life he'd walked away from trouble and controversy. Maybe he dodged issues and decisions that as skipper he should have faced. Not long before he died, in 1984, he asked me to help him write a book. He sent me a synopsis but it was too bland, too devoid of any of the sabre-rattling at Taunton. It was too gentle and jolly, consciously avoiding some of those penetrative comments that needed saying. Tim said: 'Dad once thought he'd like to be a journalist, like his old Somerset friends Ron Roberts, Bob Moore, John King and Eric Hill. The trouble was he could never have brought himself to criticise any player.' In 1960 John Arlott gave him an introduction to Guinness and he was taken on the staff. He and his family moved to Hampshire.

The warm, emotional link with Taunton was broken. That had been where he went to Priory School, influenced in cricket by one of the masters, Percy Shapland. That was where he used to play cricket with John King after Sunday School at St James's. The inner circle of friends from boyhood Taunton never much changed. That was where he was known affectionately as 'Babe' Tremlett and had his early matches with Rowbarton Brewery and Stoke St Mary. He lived less than ten minutes' walk from the county ground and would go to watch whenever he could. During schooldays, that had often meant climbing over St James's churchyard wall with his friends, to get into the ground. When it was time to leave school he worked in the offices of a local brewery and then, more to his youthful liking, he was taken on as a clerical worker by Somerset CCC. At every opportunity, he'd creep away from the ledgers to peer through the office windows as Wellard and his mates clattered along in their cricket boots to the nets. Maybe one day ...

He came out of the army to play for Somerset and his country. His final county game was in 1960 – and then it was off to sell Guinness, while also acting as an enthusiastic and efficient secretary of the local Licensed Victuallers' Association. There was more time to spend with his family. Tim was to become a Hampshire player and later their director of cricket. The other son, Jonathan, played for the county's second XI. Maurice encouraged them all to be keen golfers. He played off a handicap of five and in one memorable month holed-in-one three times. He was proud of the fact that wife Lee and all three children got down to single figures.

For someone who recoiled from contentious matters and who was wrongly accused by his prejudiced adversaries in Somerset of lacking imagination, he could spin a long, anecdotal yarn for his children. On car journeys, when they were young and naturally restless, he would hold them transfixed with graphic accounts of his supposed wartime exploits and how he took on the Germans single-handed. They all knew it was fiction and the story of the intrepid soldier, with no stripes but plenty of bravado, was no more than a requested adventure story. No-one should imply he lacked imagination.

All the family remembered different examples of his sense of humour, never too far below the surface. Lee says: 'One evening he came home from work when I was doing the ironing. Usually he'd greet me but this time not a word. No response to my questions. Then he walked out again. I asked him where he was going and he just spread his arms in a non-committal way. My reaction was that if he was off somewhere, I was going too. I grabbed my coat and followed him out. He held the passenger's door open for me. Again, completely mystified, I asked him where he was going.

'Silently he drove into the garage. 'I only came out to put the car away.' It was a dry, surreal humour.'

When Tim was still a boy, the two were having cricket practice with a tennis ball on the back lawn. 'I always wanted to bowl fast in those days and ambitiously tried a couple of bouncers. Dad's response was to rebuke me for bowling short and to say, if I did it again, he'd hit me for six.' With the precocity of youth, Tim sent down another bouncer.

'The tennis ball soared three houses down – and then we heard a great shattering of glass. Dad sheepishly went indoors. I went to the top of the garden and could see that he'd hit a conservatory. Two people were inspecting the damage, looking completely puzzled. They never did discover. But the experience put me off any future attempts to bowl too short.'

Maurice played cards, mostly crib, with an insatiable enjoyment. 'For 30 years we played twice a week,' recalls Lee. 'And I didn't even like cards.' He was a man of simple tastes. He liked dripping for breakfast and would turn down his wife's offer of a steak for beans on toast in the evening. He didn't make too much money from cricket but his testimonial, though painfully modest by today's standards, enabled him and Lee to have their own house in the village of Ruishton, a few miles from Taunton. He liked the gentle pace, taking overseas players to the Rose and Crown at nearby East Lyng, for skittles.

One of the main money-making events from Tremlett's testimonial was a celebrity soccer match at Bridgwater. The great attraction was the promised appearance of Stanley Matthews whose presence was prominently featured on the advance publicity.

Bill Andrews, who had been stationed at Blackpool during the war and had even played football alongside Matthews in one charity game, suddenly received a frantic phone call from Tremlett. 'What can I do, Bill? Stan has just contacted the county club to say he can't play after all. We've got his name plastered all over the bills.'

Andrews was to tell me: 'I phoned Stan's home in Blackpool and was informed he wasn't in. I'd heard that one before, so said who I was. And, do you know, he came on the line.' Bill's persuasive words obviously worked; Matthews arrived at Bridgwater the following evening, met Bill in a little café and pocketed "a substantial amount to cover expenses".

Tremlett was not a materialistic person. After he had moved to Hampshire he gave away an England blazer to one of the local cricket clubs in

Southampton, to help them raise funds. By then he had settled on the South coast, was elected a life member of Hampshire CCC and was privately delighted to see Tim playing championship cricket. He'd have been even more so if he had lived to see his grandson, Chris, sustaining the tradition.

All that remains is for me to analyse why Maurice Fletcher Tremlett is one of my imperishable heroes. It isn't simply because of the wickets he took in those vibrant post-war summers: there were only 351 of those after all, though he dismissed Len Hutton twice in a match, and bowled Denis Compton, his brother Leslie twice, and Jack Robertson in that wondrous debut. Latterly I saw him ambling up and bowling token off breaks which I stupidly pretended were as good as Jim Laker's. Nor was it merely those perfectly coordinated straight drives which used to tempt me regularly to position myself just yards from the sight-screen in the ideal vantage point, provided I was ready to duck. He would say he learned how to hit sixes from Wellard. 'Hit sixes back over the bowler's head. It's the safest place and the shortest route,' he assured Tim.

Well yes, maybe I was influenced by his bounce and break-backs, and his sweeping bat, an image of which should have been encapsulated and preserved for every coaching manual. But it was the man, too – his loathing of confrontation and grievances, the kind that scar so many memories in county cricket; his amiable nature and common sense, with a contempt for the trivial; his conviction that cricket needed to be entertainment even if that necessitated a calculated gamble. Team-mates liked him, but they still frowned and pondered his wisdom – and their beer money – if he chose to forego a win bonus for a first innings lead. 'Trust me,' he'd say with that deceptively deferential voice of his, 'it'll be worth it when we win the match.' He could point to some unlikely victories. Tremlett was possessed of a built-in mental calculator. Perhaps he should have majored in maths. After he had left Somerset, he annually organised a cricket match among his racing friends and others at Fovant. Almost always it produced a close and exciting finish. He manipulated that, usually without the players realising how it had been done. 'I suppose it was a case of innocent match-fixing,' I was told.

He took early retirement, already unwell, and died aged 61 from a brain tumour less than a year later. The medics had been tardy with their diagnosis and for some time, to the frustration of the family, didn't seem to know what was wrong with him. It is conceivable that his illness could be traced back to a fearful injury he received during the Bath cricket festival in 1953. He was fielding at silly point when the Kent opener Tony Woollett suddenly emerged from dour defence for an aggressive off-side drive which caught Tremlett near the eye. The ball glanced off his forehead and went on to the boundary. His sinus bone was splintered and one of his eyes partially dislodged. He was rushed to hospital and there were fears for his life. He left hospital after two months, though never to see so well again. It was his left eye that suffered and when pressed would admit: 'Something's gone from my batting – I'm not picking up the ball in the same way. I suppose I'll have to cut back on the sixes.'

Tremlett saw himself quintessentially as a village cricketer. Years ago he told me in an interview: 'To me, it's the best form, with all the ingredients for a perfect Saturday – rivalry, sportsmanship and then all into the local at the end. Do you know that my most memorable feat was for Stoke St Mary against Staple Fitzpaine, a real local battle as you can imagine. I was still a boy and I took a hat-trick. Well, a sort of one. Young and keen, I always counted how many balls I had left. And on the last ball of the over, I took a wicket. As I started my walk to fine-leg, I looked back and saw the two umpires having a chat in the middle of the pitch. They hadn't met for six months and had plenty to talk about. There was no call of 'Over' and I returned for my run-up. I immediately clean-bowled the next batsman. I had a hunch by now that the umpires might have more to chat over. They proved just as absent-minded. This time I didn't set off for fine-leg. The next batsman skied first ball and the fielder at cover point had no chance. I was away like a colt and under the ball before he'd moved. So my hat-trick came from the sixth, seventh and eighth balls.' That affection for the village game, its unpredictable charms and pastoral pleasantries, never left him. We can reasonably conclude that he was happier whacking with boyish enthusiasm into the long grass of a few dozen Somerset meadows ("I was always told to keep running until they found the ball") than coping or eavesdropping on the county game's more mean-spirited politics.

He left his beloved Somerset forty years ago. Yet around the boundaries in the West, they continue to remember him with a rare warmth. Unfulfilled he may have been, but he was a player fashioned for the fans.

ROBERT WALTER VIVIAN ROBINS

1906 - 1968

Amateur cricketer, Cambridge University, Middlesex & England.

Maybe I am allowed to begin with a slightly quirky, philosophical point. Does a hero have to be liked?

Sir Don Bradman, Wally Hammond and Ian Botham were all heroes. Our homage to them, as mighty sporting performers and sublime match winners, was afforded without reservation. The Don, most recently acknowledged by *Wisden Cricketers' Almanack* as the foremost cricketer of the 20th century, was recurrently maligned for what was perceived as the soulless nature of his batting and, more so, the frigidity of his personality. In his day, the Australian dressing room could be embarrassingly divisive. God, and his proximity to or distance from Rome, was too convenient an explanation.

Hammond, who wrongly lacked the knighthood bestowed on his great rival, could also bat with heroic magnificence. In Bristol, not so far from the soup kitchens in those bleak, haggard-faced years of the Depression in the late Twenties, he brought a discerning glow to the countenances of those who came to the county ground to watch and dote. Pallid children climbed on chairs to peer with unrestrained excitement through the lofty windows of the orphanage beyond mid-wicket. Hammond possessed, too, the good looks of the idealised idol, his muscular body sculptured from Greek marble. Team-mates were in awe of his stylish grandeur; not so many, as he seemed to become selective in his friendships and socially drifted from his fellow pros, warmed to him as a man.

'Both' has softened and mellowed, rather like one of those old, honeyed Ham-stone cottages in south Somerset where he grew up, dignified now with the wisteria restored. It was not always easy to like him, though the sycophants did, in those artificial summers when we all admired and thrilled to him so much as a player. He compounded headlines, pursued by newspapers who found daily mileage in flawed celebrity. At the same time he leaned on his ghosts, picked up his tabloid cheques and existed in a dangerous, dramatic territory of blurred images and ethics.

PLAYER'S CIGARETTES

R. W. V. ROBINS

And what of Robert Walter Vivian Robins, who for matters of instinct can never be one of my sporting favourites? Which illogical whims of justification draw him within my cherished clutch of heroes? In truth he has long been one, despite – from what I have read and been told by those who played with him or knew him well – the manner of the man and qualities which I don't readily find endearing. He was quintessentially a cold fish. He could be brusque, impatient, dismissive. It helped if you agreed with him.

I saw him play only once or twice, yet always wanted to write about him. His obituaries all referred to his dynamism and enthusiasm. No cricketer possessed of these should be lightly discarded. I suspect that few players of his era, or indeed since, expended so much mental energy in the course of a match. He was a *thinker*: and usually an adventurous one. He was angry when games petered out into draws. He challenged opposing captains to regenerate matches that were meandering to pointless finality. His rejoinders to those unimpressed by his entreaties could be ferocious. 'Robbie' was never one to pussyfoot.

We are all creatures of unforgivable prejudice. Single incidents and experiences linger for decades to cloud our judgments. When I arrived in Bristol to work for an evening paper, one of my first jobs was to interview Rachel Roberts, then with the Bristol Old Vic and appearing in Ugo Betti's *The Queen and the Rebels*, the kind of play that caused whole rows of prudish inhabitants of the city's suburbia to storm out long before the end in various guises of shock-horror. I didn't know then of Miss Roberts' reputation for a lunch-time drink, especially when more than one was being offered by a callow, hard-up young journalist from the rural West Country. We met in one of those Robinson Crusoe pubs off the cobbles of King Street near the historic Theatre Royal. And the interview, or rather a Welsh-voiced monologue of increasingly animated decibels and good humour, spiced with the spectrum of juicy adjectives one would not expect from the daughter of a Baptist minister, went on deep into the afternoon. One must be charitable; perhaps she assumed the scope of my expenses was on a civilised par with Agate, Tynan or Shulman. She offered no reciprocal drink (poorly paid provincial actors seldom did). In desperation, as I saw no immediate end to the wayward, Bacchic exercise in Italian drama, I discreetly borrowed money from a rat-catcher, friend of the King Street thespians and the morning rehearsal 'alarm clock' for Peter O'Toole, who was also in the bar. It must have been, I say in gratitude, a decent week for vermin-extermination.

Years later, when she was married to Rex Harrison, I read of Miss Roberts' drinking which may have come as a surprise to him. I could have warned him. When I interviewed and subsidised her, I was working for a paper of painfully limited resources and one shortly to fold. I enjoyed her garrulous company but she was never quite forgiven for her one-way traffic of alcoholic opportunity. My subsequent notices about her performances were inclined to be muted, sub-consciously influenced by her insensitivity to my parlous state in a Bristol pub. She was to have a miserable life and I feel some guilt.

My survey of prejudices must return to the subject of cricket. I liked the sound of Hugo Yarnold. He kept wicket well for Worcestershire and his name was hardly out of the newspapers in 1949 when he had 110 victims and his stumpings were much talked about at New Road. Then he became an umpire and took charge of three Tests. My regard for him plummeted one June day in 1960 when I had gone to Bath to report Somerset's match with Gloucestershire.

Hugo, who could be punctilious, didn't approve of the jerky bowling action of Eric Bryant, a slow left-arm spinner from Weston-super-Mare, someone trying to establish himself as a county cricketer and doing his best to model himself on Tony Lock. Yarnold called him five times, four of them in an over. It was demoralising for Bryant, a rather dour, introvert character and a chain smoker beyond compare. Team-mates said that he kept a cigarette in his mouth during the after-match shower and that he surreptitiously took a packet onto the field with him, for a furtive puff between the fall of wickets. He was an outstanding club cricketer, never once called for an illegal action as far as I know. I got on well with him and resented Hugo's summary dismissal. No doubt the dressing room got less fuggy, when after a brief career he packed his bags and walked out of the first-class game.

Nor did Bill Andrews, the Somerset all-rounder, forget or forgive. His big heart was his undoing. It served him well when he bowled into the wind; he accepted and demurred only in jest when his great pal, Arthur Wellard, had the choice of ends. He was infinitely less generous when it came to Jack 'Farmer' White, a taciturn man touched by the veneer of snobbery detectable among gentlemen agriculturists of West Somerset. White never quite knew what to make of Andrews, a gangling figure with an engaging propensity to speak out of turn. Bill was maybe not the best fielder in the Somerset side. When he put down a catch off Jack White's bowling, he was greeted with a glower. In a Bank Holiday fixture against Gloucestershire, Hammond immediately straight drove with exquisite timing. Andrews, the bowler, led the crowd's applause. White wasn't having that; he rounded on Bill and told him it was his job to take wickets and not encourage acclaim for the opposition. Andrews was to tell me: 'I never forgave him for that and refused to go to his funeral.'

Are we too rash in our prejudices? I could cite a hundred such cases: of famous cricketers who kept me waiting, as if I were the delivery man at the big house, for a promised interview – of odious and obscenely dismissive football managers. They never regained respect in my treasured store cupboard of memories.

This all brings me, by a characteristically tortuous route, to what happened on a cold, misty December Tuesday in 1959 at Avonmouth Docks. The Bristol reporters had been invited onto the banana boat Camito to meet the MCC party of 15 players who were sailing for the West Indies. Walter Robins was the manager, Peter May the captain, and the new boy was David Allen, who had only just earned a regular first team place with Gloucestershire. On his own admission, Allen's selection was something of a surprise. Was he being taken to absorb the Test atmosphere and gain experience and knowledge primarily for the future? Or might he be pitched straight in? Rapid promotion, it seems, was hardly Robins' intention.

The players had been summoned to Lord's prior to the sailing. Allen, a tidy, old-fashioned off-spinner, was diffident and impressionable.

"He looked me up and down. I'm your manager. You're Allen, are you?"

There was a nervous nod. "You won't be playing in too many games. Probably some of the minor fixtures." He paused and added: "but you'll be useful to me ... I'll be expected to speak on various occasions. And I'll need someone to whom I can hand my case." He pointed down to his brief case; he was being serious.

At Avonmouth, next day, the ship's company couldn't have been more helpful. The small library had been put aside for the impromptu press conference. This was the perfect opportunity to wish the party well, especially our own local lad. It should have been relaxed and convivial. But it was nothing of the kind.

Robins was tense and unwelcoming. 'Be quick about it. We want to be away.' And that was almost as soon as we had stepped into the library.

'Could we have a word with David Allen?'

'No, you can't. You can have a quick interview with the captain and his vice-captain, Colin Cowdrey. No-one else. And get it over as soon as you can.'

What did he think? That only May and Cowdrey could string a few articulate words together? Did he imagine our fecund intentions were to hatch a 'Bodyline on a Banana Boat' scare? That we naively thought Fred Trueman and 'George' Statham were being mentally attuned to resuscitated leg-theory, or something?

It was ludicrous and patently inhospitable. The crew didn't know what was happening. Poor Peter May, looking more than ever like a harassed sixth former, was caught up in the general tension. 'Do be as quick as you can. Please.' Trueman barely had time to put the pipe in his mouth.

Robins was not the man I had expected. He was small, fussy, of nervous energy. He looked like someone halfway between Bradman and Arthur Askey in those "I thank you" glasses. I thought back to the scampered singles for Middlesex when he was faster off the blocks than his county partner and soccer contemporary, Joe Hulme. Did he play cricket, too, without a smile?

His attitude at Avonmouth was all the more mystifying when I later discovered his relatively high-profile approach during the tour itself. It is possible he had a naturally disdainful attitude towards a polite group of provincial journalists and photographers. In the West Indies, he devoted a great deal of time talking and drinking with the press. "A bloody sight more time with them than us," said one established England player. His polished public relations helped to ensure that the end-of-term reports referred to what a successful manager he had been. It was an opinion not shared by too many of the team who felt he was needlessly remote and aloof at times.

May, later unfit and giving way to Cowdrey, had a toughness of attitude that belied the boyish short-back-and-sides demeanour. On the eve of the first

Test in Barbados, he approached Allen who had been plagued by a sore spinning finger. 'I want you to play. Can you last five days?'

'Yes'. We can only guess how much confidence that resolute response carried.

The next morning at 7.30am, when Allen was still sleeping, Robins came to his hotel room. 'I looked up from under my mosquito net and he told me he'd heard that I'd promised Peter May I was fit to play.'

'Listen,' said Walter Robins. 'I know more about sore spinning fingers than anyone and you won't last half a dozen overs. Be it on your own head.' And he flounced out, far from pleased.

Allen, aged 24 and still a novice cricketer at the more elevated levels of the game, played in all five Tests, at times with discomfiture though always with resolve. He went on to play 39 times for his country, a credit to the small grammar school of Cotham, in Bristol, from where Arthur Milton and John Mortimore also graduated.

England won that rubber in the Caribbean, by beating the West Indies at Port of Spain in the second Test. By general acclaim, especially by those close to the cradle of Lord's and who avidly read the public prints, the manager had every reason to bask in the tour. He carried out his social duties capably, looked after the administration, had wise words in players' ears – they accepted his considerable knowledge of the game – and didn't court popularity when it came to discipline.

His disciplinary measures could have a heavy, authoritarian edge. From one of the players, years later, I learned of an incident involving Harry's Bar. Robins decided to ban future visits. My team insider was to tell me with undisguised relish: 'Peter May was one who'd stand up to Robbie. He took all the players to Harry's as if to say no-one was going to tell him what to do. Brave defiance from a skipper.'

When it came to the final Test of the series, in Trinidad, the game was clearly petering out into another draw. At tea-time on the last day, Robins strongly advocated what he saw as a sporting declaration. He put it to Cowdrey but the suggestion was roundly rejected. 'We've played all this cricket and are one up. We don't intend to throw the series away in the last few hours.'

There was a pointed exchange, ending when a gruff-voiced Yorkshireman felt it would be advisable if Robins left the dressing room. Or something like that.

Walter Robins was born in 1906 and went to Highgate School, where he excelled as a cricketer. There was much of the old school about him: he knew his place socially, valued deep-rooted institutions and would pontificate with a haughtiness that discounted a second point of view. Often, it must be said, he was right. His persona, though, was forever a paradox. He would have been at home in the Victorian days when the hansoms rattled along St John's Wood

Road. He would equally have argued that he was in many ways a modernist. He was not against change if he thought it benefited the game. In committee, he could be positively radical, or at least sound that way. He worried about falling gates and ill-conceived trends.

In 1963, five years before Robins' death, Geoffrey Howard, then the secretary of Lancashire CCC, wrote to him as an *eminence grise* and someone with the game very much at heart. Howard had various concerns, including the need to revive spectator interest. He had noted in alarm the fall in attendances at the two Lancashire-Australia matches in 1956. He listed what he thought was wrong and hoped there would be a reply. It came at some length under the note-heading of Stafford Knight & Co Ltd (Insurance Brokers), of Fenchurch Street, London EC3.

> ... I quite agree with you about seam bowling and the one reason why I try to avoid ordinary first class matches in the way I do is because of this eternal type of bowling, with the wicket keeper always standing back.
>
> One new ball per innings would suit me, provided it only applies to the county championship. I feel that visitors to this country should play under the laws of cricket and I can't see a change in the New Ball affecting teams overseas. I would also try to amend the law whereby there should be no rubbing at all of the ball, let alone using hair oil. I also think the average bowler runs too far – surely 20 yards is enough.
>
> I don't know why you have written to me on this point because my name isn't Mr Cricket. However, I take it as a compliment and I can assure you the points which you have raised are very much in the legislators' minds at the moment.
>
> Regarding our very successful meeting at Lord's the other day, the only thing that worried me was the pooling of the gates, because I visualise poor old Middlesex coming out from it the worst of all the counties. Admittedly we always have a good date for the match against the Tourists but on the other hand, other than MCC, we give the Tourists the best return ...

The letter revealed much about Robins: the way he was thinking incessantly about cricket, the rights and wrongs, the changes that were needed. Bowlers' long runs clearly irritated him. There was also the pleasant touch of modesty, even if we suspect he privately considered himself one of the game's eminent authorities.

We must not ignore his own playing career. There were the runs and wickets for Highgate after receiving his earliest coaching from his father who had played at times for Staffordshire. He won his Blue as a fresher at

Cambridge, played in two more Varsity matches and scored a hundred against Oxford in his third year, when he also took eight wickets.

His first game for Middlesex was while he was still at school. The county career spanned from 1925-51 and he made 258 appearances. There were 19 Tests and 64 Test wickets. He toured Australia 1936-37 as vice captain to Gubby; his one century for his country was against South Africa at Old Trafford in 1935. He was in jaunty form and took only just over two hours. In all he scored 13,884 runs, including 11 hundreds, and took 969 wickets. His first full season with Middlesex was 1929. He was a bandy-legged batsman of impish endeavour and a bowler of twitching fingers and unreliable length. In that memorable summer he completed his only double. The papers were full of his cheekiness and said he would go on to lead his county. So he did from 1935-38 and again after the war when they won the championship in 1947. He captained England three times. But, oddly, he was never president of MCC. 'Most presidents were Old Etonians,' someone told me. Robbie's son, Charles, who played 44 times for Middlesex, did go to Eton.

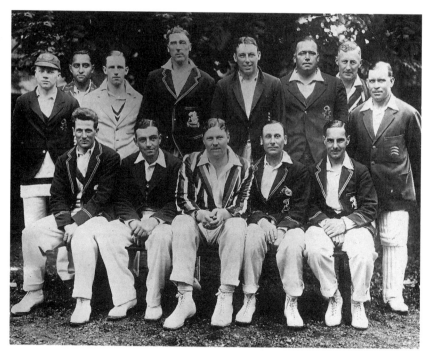

England 1930

back: *Duckworth, Duleepsinjhi, Robins, Woolley,*
          Tate, Tyldesley (R), White, Hendren
front: *Larwood, Hammond, Chapman, Hobbs, Sutcliffe*

Dudley Carew, in *To The Wicket*, probably got Walter Robins as well as anyone. "He was quick, short, with the walk and build of a cavalry man and a manner of batting most commonly described as cheeky ... it was capricious, volatile, sometimes match-winning, sometimes disappointing, always individual. As a bowler he was much the same."

As a fielder he was happiest in the covers. He could also be scathing about lapses in the field. During one match in the 1959-60 Test series in the West Indies, he told three of the team that they were the worst on the off-side he'd ever seen. 'I was one of them,' joked David Allen recently. It seemed a harsh judgment. Allen may occasionally have given the impression of a lackadaisical manner as he strolled the outfield; but he had a deadly return, and batsmen were perhaps deceived by that hint of somnolence.

Robbie's leg breaks and googlies shimmered with experiment and could be devalued by carelessness. He hated to dawdle as a batsman; the restless footwork was no more than one would expect from a footballer who played at inside forward for Cambridge and had a few games for Nottingham Forest. Like many serious men, he flirted with showmanship when he had a bat in his hand. Denzil Batchelor, the cricket writer, went to the extreme of calling him 'a card'. That, I feel, goes too far.

He ran Middlesex as secretary from 1935-50 always efficiently, not always engagingly. Above all, he was respected. So he was as a Test selector, and chairman. He spoke his piece forcefully; he knew no other way. There was an undeniable logic behind many of his ideas, however dogmatically they were expressed.

The pros could never quite make up their minds about him. Bill Bowes would refer to the "cocky robin" approach RWV had when dancing down the pitch. Andy Wilson, the little wicket keeper, started at Lord's before joining Gloucestershire in the mid-30s. He was in the team which went back to play Middlesex and in a stage whisper as Wilson walked to the wicket, Robins said: 'This little 'un won't be around for long – he's only a rabbit.'

Andy, gentle and compliant by nature, resented what he saw as a slur. Before long he was leaning back to hook Robbie for six in the best Hendren tradition, and progressed with much merit to his hundred. On his way back to the pavilion, he did a detour by way of the Middlesex captain. 'Not bad for a rabbit was it, Mr Cock Robin.'

That was a sparky, untypical reaction from Wilson. I have a suspicion that Robins, however much he recommended a measure of subservience from the less distinguished professionals, would have understood. He approved of aggression in our sporting deeds and so would have appreciated the small left-hander's need to fight back.

I come back to my original point. How much are we really expected to like our heroes?

I had just left school. My head and nostrils were full of romantic dreams and printer's ink - and I was ready to embrace a dozen heroes.

Some of them were legendary Fleet Street figures. I doted on them, disregarding slovenly syntax, as I read those short, pithy paragraphs of human interest. All I wanted was slavishly to clone their styles and the way they dressed. Most of them seemed to wear trilbies; dutifully, I bought a brown one and must have been the only 16-year-old in my hometown to wear a triby to work. It was not ideal headwear on my four-mile cycle ride from home each morning. In the winter months, as I freewheeled at a frantic pace down Hendford Hill, my hat would come off at least once a week. On one occasion it blew across the road and onto the single-track railway line. I retrieved it by sliding down the steep embankment in undignified embarrassment. If it occurred to me that Harry Procter, Arthur Helliwell and other London by-line practitioners were more likely to arrive at their office in a taxi, I conveniently blotted the incongruous comparison from my mind.

Times were bleak just after the war. Austerity was manifested in the drab demob suits, the weary eyes of disillusioned soldiers trying to reorientate to times that, at least in theory, offered them a better, more liberated chance in life. We were also bombarded by the incessant reminders on the wireless and in the shop windows that almost everything was in short supply.

Sport was a wonderful antidote. We crowded the football terraces and the cricket boundaries. Here was the semblance of glamour and excitement that life so palpably lacked. We had moved on from Churchill to Compton and Edrich. In Yeovil, there was for me Alec Stock. He had come, an unknown West Countryman, to my local football club as manager. My idolatry was rapid - and remote. I would see him walking to the bank - with the Saturday takings, I assumed - and I stayed on the other side of the road. He wasn't yet 30 and appeared rather like a good looking bank manager himself. The limp in his stride hardly suggested an athletic career. I used to think how neat his appearance was; how serious, too. There was invariably a preoccupied expression, as if he was already formulating how his team of part-timers would line up for their next Southern League encounter.

I didn't yet cover football for my weekly paper. But over the next few years I felt I knew most of the players intimately. I would go to the Wellington Inn for my half-pint of strong cider, simply to be served by Nick Collins, Yeovil's wing-half and captain. I would stroll along Wyndham Street, close to my office, in the hope of spying Les Blizzard, the lean, wan centre-half, buying his fish and chips at Beswick's. Les lived on them and the thick batter and greasy chips (we weren't yet obsessed with irritating dietary whims in those early post-war years) had no obvious detrimental effect on the phlegmatic manner he stifled opposing centre forwards of more formidable physique.

But Stock was special. I was still ingenuous and unworldly, with scant knowledge of the game's history and stereotypes. I did know, however, that player-managers at the level of association football that I watched on the emerald slopes at Huish were usually wizened old campaigners with gruff, regional accents, as well as a basic vocabulary spiced with versatile present participles transformed lazily into adjectives whose origins were more akin to sexual functions.

Stock did not conform to any of this. He had just come out of the army, a quiet-spoken officer who had been a successful tank commander in Cromwells and been wounded near Caen. The Mendip vowels could barely be detected, only then in moments of stress. He had a trim, civilised presence, maybe viewed just a trifle suspiciously by sections of South Somerset's rural proletariat. They didn't realise that he was the son of a miner, and was already someone who had experienced both sides of the social divide.

During his three years at Yeovil I watched and admired him constantly: often from behind the goal at the Bruttons end, sometimes perched precariously on a stray beer crate to gain me inches. Huish had a reassuring, distinctive smell as we sniffed the malt that wafted over from the nearby brewery. It added to the sheer intoxication of the mood. But I also saw him at work before, during and after the game. He seemed to be doing everything - mixing the concrete, marking the pitch, cutting the grass and, of course, exhorting his players in persuasive, well-enunciated tones. I also noticed that he was still frequently in his suit ten minutes before kick-off, sorting out ticket queries and other unscheduled administrative complications. All that for £500 a year.

I don't believe I harboured any specific literary aspirations in those days, outside the services of the Fourth Estate. Yet I was probably well qualified to be Stock's Boswell. Without having actually spoken to him at all, I observed his working methods with a fledgling reporter's acute eye. What was obvious was that he had an innate organisational ability and never recoiled from making decisions. It was something, I came to realise, that emanated from the difficult days when he had to improvise as an army officer. At Yeovil Town FC his board of directors, an unwieldy number, glovers and grocers, let him get on with the football. They interfered only in the unimportant facets and he privately accepted that was their prerogative.

Gradually he may have recognised me as a callow copy-boy on the local paper. My regard for him kept its distance. When he sent the occasional note to my sports editor, I was transfixed by the handsome handwriting, so much so that I attempted to copy it. If this was the hand of a former trainee bank clerk, there seemed a strong case for me to put in a job application to the nearest Barclay's. Over those three seasons I gained confidence and a little stature. After the match I now began to go with my journalistic superiors into the steamy changing-rooms. The claustrophic ablutions had their own rough-and-ready convivial charm. As the steam wreathed its way out through the half closed door, seeking minute cracks in the window panes, big naked bodies, freed of 90 minutes' endeavour and the caking mud of the battlefield,

emerged from the hissing haze. They were ready for the mugs of strong, sugary tea that Stan, the trainer, poured from his chipped enamel pot. It was an unself-conscious business; the scene was as asexual as school showers used to be after cross-country.

By then, Stock was already changed and was counting the money in his adjoining minuscule office. 'What d'you think about that one then, Alec!' And he would politely break off. 'Seventeen pounds, thirteen and sixpence - em, what was that? Ah well, yes, we just about deserved it. Young Ralph had a blinder, didn't he? Some club will be knocking on his door at Stock-under-Ham before long if he carries on like that ...'

I would stand back in the doorway, inhibited, in awe. I imagined I was in the presence of Herbert Chapman. Stock had been chosen from 60 applicants for the post, which incorporated being the secretary as well as player-manager. That measured conversational authority would have entranced them at the interview.

By his third year in the job, he had taken his team to the fifth round of the FA Cup. Bury and vaunted Sunderland had toppled in the process. This was soccer history. Yeovil was no longer merely an aircraft factory and the place where they made gloves. It was now the most famous non-League club in the country, with even its own fan club in America.

The win over Sunderland remains the nonpareil of my sporting life. I had been there, running and dictating copy for others from a butcher's shop, savouring the glimpses of my green-shirted gladiators on each return to the reverberating, fog-shrouded ground. I joyously experienced the two Yeovil goals and every heroic assault on the Sunderland goal through the noble clichés that I relayed to half a dozen London offices with inordinate pride. My tentative teenage voice took on the suitably sonorous grandeur of an exalted wordsmith for the occasion.

Soon, as I had increasingly feared, Alec was gone. He was no more the archetypal manager on the day he left than when he arrived. For three years he had learnt his trade and was now ready for the League, first with Leyton Orient. My father ran a small market garden in those days and he gave me some begonias as a parting present for Alec and his wife, Marjorie. Too shy to hand them over, I left them with a brief note in his office.

On the most slender of evidence, conflicting with what I have just written about my unequivocal boyish appraisal of him in footballing terms, I still remain convinced that he should have been a county cricketer. His affection for the summer game never wavered. Years later, as we talked at one of the pubs near Peasedown St. John, where he was born, he confided how much he would have liked to play for Somerset. He was a fine, natural cricketer, captaining his grammar school at cricket (and rugby) and having one highly promising season with Midsomer Norton, a top-class Somerset club side, just before the war. He was an orthodox batsman, eager to go for his shots even though handicapped by a broken wrist which had never quite mended. He was also an excellent cover point, with safe hands and an unbridled penchant to parade the off-side arc and chase to his left to cut off those intended square-cut fours. "As young club cricketers we always hoped that someone from the county might be watching." Bill Andrews did once or twice, and very much liked what he saw. But he was only a player himself then; by the time he had been appointed coach, the war had come and gone. Stock was now a limping footballer.

One of Alec Stock's last cricketing appearances, at Weston-super-Mare
Standing: the author, David Solomons, novelist Derek Robinson,
Peter Davies, Alec Stock, Lew Clark, Terry Bush
Kneeling: George Petherbridge, David Allen (ex Glos & England),
actor Trevor Bannister, TV presenter Bruce Hockin

I have repeatedly been surprised to hear professional footballers, in confidential asides, tell how much more they would have liked to play cricket for a living. John Atyeo was one of Bristol City's most famous players, talented enough to play six times for England. His father, a railwayman, was delighted at such acclaim and yet couldn't wholly conceal his disappointment. All he'd wanted was for Big John, the village boy of bounteous athletic gifts, to be a Somerset all-rounder. Little Fanny Walden was happier fielding in the covers for Northants than chasing down the wing for Spurs. Successful footballers like Joe Hulme, Sam Weaver, Les Berry and Arthur Milton all, I suspect, preferred cricket: and there were a hundred others, right up maybe to Gary Lineker. If only there hadn't been such a vast financial imbalance.

Stock suffered badly from asthma in later life. His solicitous wife didn't approve of him playing any more. So he would secrete his flannels and boots in the boot of his car before driving off to pick up his great friend Ted Drake, who earlier played for Hampshire when not taking a battering as he marauded with verve and courage through the middle for Arsenal. I was lucky enough to play in the last two matches that Stock and Drake appeared together. One was at Clarence Park, Weston-super-Mare's former county venue, fringed by the pines and just up the road from the seafront. It was a centenary game for Somerset in 1975 and 5000 came to watch. Alec was wheezing badly, I remember, as he stooped to field the ball, flawlessly as ever, on the off side. Something else I noticed was the pristine condition of the pair's kit. Old pros don't dress down. They wear the uniform of their trade with a timeless pride.

In the summer months when he lived at Epsom, Stock was persuaded to do some umpiring. More recently and with equal enthusiasm, he did the same at his native Peasedown. By then he was a widower, living with his daughter in Bournemouth, travelling regularly back to Peasedown to place flowers on the grave of his wife and his parents. He loved the Red Post ground. At the time of the General Strike, his father had been one of the unemployed miners who helped to lay the original square. By tradition, Peasedown men had thick muscles and knew the way to sweat: it was better sweating in the open air.

By the 1990s, the village had a fine, thriving club, running three weekend sides, one for Wednesday and two youth elevens. He came to watch and applaud from the boundary. There was some kind of philosophical fulfilment when, back on his native soil, he was asked to adjudicate. He showed no levity or bias, although according to one fellow parishioner "he always wanted to see Peasedown win." But he was never a rabid partisan; he would spontaneously murmur his congratulations to a batsman, of either side, if the stroke was a handsome, attacking one. He'd played a few matches for the village years before. When Ken Willcox, the present chairman, was away doing his National Service and Peasedown were playing in a cricket knock-out final, his father spotted Alec on the boundary. He rushed home, picked up Ken's shirt and flannels and handed them to a nonplussed Stock. The late choice did rather well. He was a nominal member of the club in any case - and there were no repercussions.

Over the years I got to know Alec better than when he administered with that permanently perplexed brow and distinctive *élan* at Yeovil. In our varying ways we had something in common. We were both village boys in our hearts, both our parents' only child. We were curious and inquisitive about what went on around us. We had similar values. Like most of the boys in my village I sang in the choir three times every Sunday. We were not so much seduced by the words from the pulpit; we did our choral duty to please our parents and, in my case, to earn three-and-sixpence a quarter. The pears, suspended so enticingly from the slip arms of their branches on the wall of the kitchen garden alongside the churchpath were another seasonal attraction. Alec grew up in a mining community where so often the chapels outnumbered the pubs and where best suits were obligatory on Sunday. As he recalls, the men didn't even cut a cabbage on the Sabbath. Alec went to church in the morning, attended Sunday School in the afternoon and genuinely enjoyed the Methodist evenings "because the singing was so good".

Peasedown St. John is a long way from Loftus Road, Highbury and Roma, three of his ports of professional call. The village is functional, its cottages and little terrace houses daubed by the greyness that symbolises the community's past deprivations. When he motors home, with the wreaths and the memories of youth, he pulls in the car and gazes across the vast, haughty undulations of the Mendips. This is where he comes to reminisce: about those little, isolated homesteads and the families who once lived there, below in the valleys. 'Look, down there, see that house, that's where ...' He points out, with an almost unspoken eloquence, the sites, now verdant, of the numerous pits that used to scar this sublime landscape. He reminds you it's birdnesting time and those were the lanes where once he went in search of eggs. He shows you the three woods where he played, the direction of the best chestnut trees; the knowledge of natural history he acquired in the exciting process of self-discovery is apparent in a sustained, enthusiasm for the countryside.

His mother had eight brothers and three sisters. All the brothers were miners; virtually every man in the parish was. They would come up on the early cage on a Saturday morning. The flush of expectancy was defiantly visible through the caked grime on their faces. The brothers lived more or less next door to each other. Their shift finished, they would tear off their blackened clothes in the backyards. Then, as part of an uplifting ritual, they'd move into the kitchen. The water was warm, waiting for them in the tin bath in front of the roaring fire. Around the fire was positioned the polished brass guard and on it were the football shirts, red and yellow, aired and ironed. The brothers would pull on their shirts, already in spirit out on the field, their increasing animation offsetting aching limbs from their subterranean labours. Kitted out and clean, they'd sit down to dinner. "A proper knife and fork job," as Alec recalls.

Peasedown Miners played in the Western League. They were big and strong: and notorious. It was said oppositions needed to be equally fearless to play against them. The Miners were rejuvenated by the soap suds and a good meal; they were now ready to do battle. It was for most of them the highlight of their week. Saturday's fixture was the way to spit the coal dust out of their lungs - and make their aggressive statement in the pure air, after being cramped and cowed in the belly of the scarred Mendip hills. In Stock's words: 'They were like birds set free.' In one of the local pubs hangs a photograph of a victorious Peasedown team. The caption graphically tells us that every player came from within a mile of the nearest local pit.

This was Stock's first club, certainly in affection. His father was on the committee. He himself marked the pitch on Saturday mornings. The family involvement was extended to his mother who made two big enamel cans of coffee for the teams at half-time. Alec would run home to collect them; his father would hand one to the visitors and Alec, with his little strides and a sheepish grin that reflected importance and pride, would take the other can to the home side. His reward was a generous measure of coffee, poured into the lid for him by the goalkeeper. The pattern didn't change. In those more basic days, the players never left the field at the interval. There was precious little shelter for them if it was raining, and it was too far to troop back to the pub which served as their changing-room.

He was devoted to his parents who made willing sacrifices for him. Their abiding resolve was the he should never go down the pits. He won his scholarship at the village school and wondered what his future might be. Children left their fathers to worry about the ominous political implications of the times. His father was 'dead Labour'; they all were. Peasedown had an insular communal warmth, a defiant independence of spirit, and he liked that.

The General Strike brought much hardship to villages like Peasedown, where life revolved round one industry. Families had difficulty feeding and looking after their children. A cousin was sent to stay with friends in Dartford, Kent. Alec's father and uncle, both out of work, followed to Dartford and their families later joined them. Alec was sent to the local grammar school, making academic and, more so, sporting progress. He stayed there at school until he was seventeen and then took a banking job in the City. That pleased his father and mother.

He may have excelled as a fly-half or centre for his school but his football also had a discernible maturity about it. Deftly he learned to combine trial matches with late-night overtime at the bank for half-a-crown a time. He was snatching a trial for Spurs when an imposing grey-haired man with a lovely County Durham accent was standing on the touchline. 'You must come and join us at Charlton,' said Jimmy Seed. He didn't only sign Alec but his father as well. Seed, ever susceptible to the plight of miners, took the father on as assistant groundsman at The Valley. It was worth £3-10s a week 'and was the best, happiest job Dad ever did.' So by 1936 young Stock was a professional footballer. He would be staying above ground.

By the time the war came he had moved to Queen's Park Rangers, the club he was later to take from the third to the first division, and to victory in the League Cup final at Wembley. The war took almost six and a half years of his life. He had wanted to join the Somerset Light Infantry ("to be among my own") but to his confusion was put into the Yorkshire Regiment and sent to Plymouth. A commission followed and he was posted to the 2nd Northamptonshire Yeomanry, in tanks. His wounding left him partially deaf and with the limp which he did his best to disguise now as a composed, scheming and gentle-paced inside forward for Yeovil.

He took to army life and argued it was the perfect preparation for someone with ambition to be a football manager. He saw the barrack room as an extension of the dressing-room - 'just a load of blokes talking about fitness, tactics and the best way to win'. His job as an officer was to get maximum response from his men. Here were invaluable lessons in human nature. As an erstwhile village boy, he came to appreciate the qualities of the public school types he met in the Services, 'the way they could lead'.

He liked taking on responsibility himself. That was demonstrably true during more than 35 years in football management. Whenever a club, like Arsenal for instance, tended to dilute his power, he bristled. He was angered by decisions to which he was not privy. In the army, the decisions were increasingly his. When one day his Commanding Officer said to him: 'Let's see, Alec, you're from Bath, aren't you? We've got a young fellow coming up on a court martial. Comes from Bristol. I'm sure you'd like to defend him'. Lieut. Stock took a sharp intake of breath and nodded. 'Here's the book and his records. Read it up - it's quite easy.' And that was how, for the only time, he found himself in the onerous role of advocate. He put up a strong, well reasoned and, no doubt affectionate, case for his fellow West Countryman.

Over his varied life - as miner's son, trainee banker, soldier and soccer manager - Stock was full of contradictions. He was a shy, gentle man who loved the solitude of gardening. Back at Peasedown, he'd learnt how to plant potatoes and hoe between the onion lines. When he lived near Wimborne, in the post football days, his family would peer through the kitchen window and see how contented he was on a summer's evening, digging and cultivating his vegetable garden. 'Please, Dad ... please ... no more runner beans,' his daughters would implore.

But, just occasionally, there was the explosive side to him. At more than one of his league clubs he would stand up to an irritating director he felt had a negligible understanding of the game and the needs of the boardroom. Directors who made fatuous remarks and took snide digs at him were his bêtes noires. He used to tell me: 'They came into the clubs as businessmen and maybe they were reasonably good at that. Yet in footballing terms, they were little children.'

He was a devoted family man, full of love for Marjorie and his daughters, Elizabeth and Sarah, all of whom were school teachers. But he went on holiday with them less frequently than they would have liked. He didn't much enjoy holidays; he'd see the family off at the airport and then motor to the football club, wander into his office and place a blank piece of paper on his desk. The summer months, he used to say, were when the work was really done. That was when he could doodle on that piece of paper, work out experimental formations and decide how best he could win matches from his existing staff. Like too many managers, obsessed with their jobs, he was inevitably inclined to be sexist. Marjorie complained good-naturedly that he never phoned to say when he was coming home for his supper (he ate only one proper meal a day in any case). Once she sallied into print, in a not entirely tongue-in-cheek adjunct to a book he was writing, to say he was so introspective and preoccupied during his Yeovil months that she almost hoped he would break a leg and so take a few weeks off.

Alec and Marjorie on their wedding day

In the Somerset mining tradition he could also be cussed. During all the successes that came QPR's way under his perspicacious managership, no-one ever once thanked him. Such a lack of gratitude, even common courtesy, simmered away in his psyche. Social graces were formulated by his duties in the City bank and then the Officer's Mess. Long before, the please-and-thank you culture had been instilled in him by his parents. The lapses in reasonable behaviour, from certain members of the boardroom, upset him. And he would let them know.

So he did, in his own way, to trusted aides Les Gore and Nick Collins, whom he had brought with him to Leyton from Yeovil. Orient were on top of the table, away to Gillingham. They were, in Stock's words, the Littlewoods away banker of the day. But in the immediate build-up he refused to take anything for granted; he reiterated the dangers in a monologue to the pair that seemed to go on for ever.

He was walking behind Gore and Collins as they went onto the field before the kick-off. 'Les suddenly turned round and told me I got on his bloody nerves. And Nick, who was never lost for a word, suggested that I should bugger-off and leave them alone.' He hadn't had that kind of ultimatum before, certainly not from mates.

'All right. Sod you, I will.' Alec stopped in his tracks, turned and walked out of the ground. He went to the cinema instead.

He had the last resounding laugh. Leyton won 3-0. And the Sunday papers gave him all the credit for adeptly turning things round with a masterly half-time talk …

He was both a pragmatist and a wily psychologist. During that historic Cup win over Sunderland, Yeovil were tensely hanging onto their slender lead in extra time. When the ball came to Stock, he jettisoned every shred of subtlety and heaved it high over the stand and probably through the lofty Victorian windows of the adjoining junior school. Sunderland's most famous player, Len Shackleton, whose normally extrovert dexterity had been obscured by the unceremonious attentions of Stock and Bob Keeton, the commercial traveller from Devon, followed the flight of the disappearing ball and said with some irony: 'What d'you do that for? Don't spoil a good game.'

The psychological skills were demonstrated in his affable manipulation of the reporters, causing Bury and Sunderland in turn to fear a Huish slope that took on Alpine proportions. Later came the deft way he handled players like Rodney Marsh and Stan Bowles. 'Rodney was absolutely no problem for me - and what a goal rate! Just once I said to him, "Rodney, we run in this club, you know." He got the message.' Bowles had his detractors, of course, but Stock was not among them. Stan told his manager that people saw him as a footballer who gambled. Not true at all. He was a gambler who played a bit of football. The old White City entrance was only a few hundred yards from the QPR ground. On the return from away games, Stock would arrange for the team coach to stop first at the White City to drop off Bowles. The player with the suspect reputation could have asked for no more.

Stock was a great talker: on soccer tactics, man management, on how to grow runner beans. Once or twice he drove Gore and Collins to distraction. Mostly he talked a common sense nurtured on the green pitted hills of North Somerset. It wasn't in the nature to be egotistical. But he was invariably worth listening to. He had this tendency to make a shrewd subjective point and then look up, above his glass of regional bitter, for confirmation. Those were the kind of inner thoughts that he dispensed as he picked with nominal interest at his modest pub meal. I knew he had bought Marsh for £15,000 and later, Malcolm Macdonald for £17,000 (sold on to Newcastle for £180,000 from Luton).

> I must admit I liked buying and selling, helped by managing clubs at the lower levels. Always good at figures, you know. Had to be as secretary at Yeovil. But being a secretary isn't difficult. Nor is coaching. The difficult bit is managing - employing the right staff, signing the right players. I quite enjoyed the eternal struggles. And I quickly learnt the only thing many directors could understand was the result, whether we won or lost. The number one requirement of a manager is being able to pick a team, something as fundamental as that.

You're confronted by a blank sheet of paper. Anyone can put down eleven names on it. The secret is to find the right blend and balance. And I always liked to have someone in the club I could bounce ideas off. Management is also about knowing how to talk to people. It was my job to know every single thing about the club and the individual players. That often included their wives and families as well. It was important that the players liked me as well as respected me. Do you know that during my 35 years in football management - is that a record? - I never had one of my players sent off. For my part, I never suspended or fined one. Tempers were bound to get a bit frayed on occasions. These were grown men in a confined dressing room after all. We aren't talking of "Kiss in the Ring"! So-called player power was never the remotest problem for me. In football clubs, remember, you have a marvellous group called senior pros. A whisper about a tricky player goes down the line to them (note the military imagery that he repeatedly used in his conversation). 'The senior pros would say: "Leave it to us"; it didn't need to be sorted out in my office. At the same time, I couldn't expect 30 blokes always to be the best of pals. If I saw a couple of them having a dust-up, I'd tell the others that if they tried to stop it, I'd give them the sack. What I was implying was that those two at each other's throat should get it out of their system. My intention was to have my club well organised. Players responded to that. Everything was in order for them and they sensed that they belonged to a bloody good club. I built up relationships and formed conclusions all the time. Long ago I discovered that what a player was like on the field was what he was like off it - or the other way round. A grafter was a grafter. The spiv never changed, whether or not he had a football shirt on.

There, in relatively few lines, is enough wisdom to form the basis of a weekend seminar. Another equally comprehensive one could revolve round his tactical notions. He was a 4-4-2 man, even on that heady and overcast day when, four years after the war, Sunderland were calmly out-manoeuvred by a young tank commander. Stock believed in reliable front men. The leggy Ray Wright and Eric Bryant, in their uncomplicated ways, did it for him at Huish. More grandly, so did Rodney and Les Allen for QPR, Macdonald and Givens for Luton.

It would be wrong to say that the pattern was exclusively smooth. The feathers could be ruffled; he'd dig his heels in over a principle. He took QPR to the first division for the first time in their history. It was a moment for celebration and expectations. But he had chosen to leave, after an internecine exchange or two, before a match could be played at the higher level with him in charge. In 1956 he became assistant manager to Tom Whittaker at Highbury. Some saw subsequent elevation to the plush, exalted chair at

Arsenal, as a formality. It was nothing of the kind. He stayed for 53 days, confused and frustrated by a role that carried risible authority. Two hours of coaching each morning with supercilious players, some of whom paid him only token attention, was to him a criminal waste of time. The club even told him he was too conscientious and that he should wander off at noon for a round of golf. He saw little of the desk-bound Whittaker; once when he unreservedly admonished a sulking player, the supposedly avuncular Tom failed to support him. He decided that it was better to be back with self-effacing Orient, although their chairman rushed prematurely into print to tell the world. Back page headlines in the *Standard* hastened an unedifying parting from Highbury.

A year later he was off again, this time to Roma. Maybe for the only time in his rational life he was partially seduced by the glamorous portents. His friends, those who knew him best, would have told him it would never work. Latin intrigue was more than a foreign language. They didn't even allow him into the boardroom. The directors and other hangers-on had more intimacy with the players than he. He was left to find accommodation for his wife and two young daughters. Officially he was team manager of A.S. Roma: but it could have fooled him. In matters of control he was no more than a peripheral figure. He was gone, and back to Brisbane Road, inside four months. The pampered team, it should be said, lost only once while he was there. There was no regret from Stock about terminating his Italian employment so abruptly. One suspects there may have been, at least in retrospect, about his leaving Arsenal.

In the West Country tradition he was a sentimental man. That was no doubt why he went back twice as manager of Leyton Orient, why he returned to QPR as a director. Perhaps he was a restless man, ever ready to try a new club when the last one was starting to creak acrimoniously. Within that crowded, sagacious and occasionally impulsive life, he was also manager at Luton - he guided them to promotion - Fulham, the team he took to the 1975 cup final, and Bournemouth.

Above all he was liked by his players. A few of them, like Bobby Moore (at Fulham), Marsh and Bowles, were stars; the majority were honest jobbing footballers. It is in no sense derogatory to say he excelled in extracting the best out of teams at the lower level. He inspired Orient to beat Everton in the Cup: not quite a surprise of Sunderland magnitude but still a fine, sweaty triumph.

Some managers, with limited vocabularies and barren personalities, loathe the public relations work that goes remorselessly with the job. Stock relished it. He ran up Fleet Street phone bills, providing angles for the tabloids as well as reasoned analysis when it was requested. He was always available to a reporter - and that meant, to his wife's despair, on a Sunday. He motored hundreds of miles to give talks to village football and cricket clubs and to sit on sports panels. That he called his "missionary work".

But former managers in old age, when their much loved wives and good friends like Ted Drake have died, become lonely men. They miss the banter of the dressing rooms, the gossip, the preoccupation with fitness. No longer have they contemporaries, who live nearby, with whom they can swap stories of past battles. In one poignant moment, Alec told me on the phone: 'I'm going to the dentist next Tuesday. It's an event in the week, something to look forward to.'

In more recent times he has motored along to watch Swanage Town, just down the road, and more often Yeovil Town, where he continues to be treated like a revered elder statesman. There have been treasured moments when he has sat in the clubhouse at Peasedown, still in his white umpire's coat, with half a guilty, unseasonal eye on the TV set, while an Italian soccer match is being enacted. Young Mendip cricketers crowd round him. 'You must know all about those Eye-tie clubs, Alec.' He nods; in those strange, misplaced, alien weeks with Roma, he found time to absorb what seemed like a lifetime's education on Italian geography, attitudes and professional sport. He preferred the geography to the football.

His health has not been so good in recent years, though the memories and the measured words of reflection and counsel are as vivid and telling as ever. Rodney Marsh was the special guest at a testimonial dinner for Alec, held early in 2000 at Yeovil. It was an evening of much good nature and tongue-in-cheek joviality. Rodney recalled a distant season when Queen's Park Rangers could do no wrong as he kept scoring goals. *The People* had rung him and promised £500 for a story if he would say that he should be playing for England. He decided to ask Stocky's permission and was advised that it would do him no favours with the England manager. On the Sunday he bought *The People* to discover a piece from Alec Stock with a screaming headline RODNEY SHOULD BE PLAYING FOR HIS COUNTRY.

We can't be sure if the cheque was shared or even if the delightful story was true. Yet it conveys the warm, jokey relationship Stock had with his players.

All these years after, I continue to see him, in my mind's eye, dapper in appearance, solemn of face, never lacking an old-world courtesy when a stranger with a market-day accent wishes him good-morning, walking briskly down to the bank in Yeovil's pale winter sun; or maybe knocking on the solicitor's door, just over the cobbles from the parish church, to tell the gawky Dickie Dyke, the office boy, that he'd be needed to play against Sunderland but it wouldn't affect his bible-class attendance the following day. Alec was a man for all seasons and occasions.

*Alec Stock (seated) with Eric Bryant, the two scorers
in Yeovil's F.A. Cup triumph over Sunderland*

ALFRED ERNEST DIPPER

1885 - 1945

Gloucestershire farmer's son and batting stalwart.

It was sometimes said, usually and wisely out of his hearing, that Alf Dipper had the most inelegant stance and style in county cricket. The off drive, for instance, so fashionable and aesthetically pleasing, was anathema to him. Whenever he could, which might be every ball in an over, he would twist his sturdy, stained old bat and pull to leg.

Old Dip – and in truth he always looked old, never sprightly – would stand no more than half upright, singularly awkward and ill balanced. The feet were comfortably though wrongly positioned, while his protruding bottom stretched almost all the way, it seemed, to the square-leg umpire. That was how it had been for him, as long as anyone could remember. He was never too bothered by the entreaties of successive coaches; he was an endearing, cussed countryman who got on with his cricket in his own way, ignoring the surfeit of counsel extended to him with declining hope of its making any real impression. The undeniable fact was that in his rural operation of putting bat to ball, devoid of irksome refinement, he seldom played a streaky shot. He might shuffle across the crease and to the irritation of countless bowlers obscure his stumps at some point. Yet with dogged resolve, he instinctively moved to the pitch of the ball. Little passed his bat.

No one in the Gloucestershire club attempted too hard to change him. Why should they? He was utterly reliable as he was. For some years he carried the county's threadbare batting on his artisan shoulders. He scored 53 hundreds, five times passed 2000 runs in a season, and played once for England. What conceivable case could be made out for revising his practical, if unsightly, methods of batsmanship?

He was a farmer's son, one of ten children. He went to the village school at Apperley, a few miles from Tewkesbury, and one suspects he was happier playing embryonic cricket in the long grass of the parish than cleaning out the cow stalls, though his adolescent muscles were doubtless strengthened by the obligatory stints in the hayfield and at harvest time.

The family lived at Green Farm, opposite the village pond where the moorhens continue so decorously to congregate. For Alf, the cricket field was just half a mile down the lane. At the turn of the century and in the next few years when he played for Apperley, the ground was devoid of any manicured grandeur. There were undulations, molehills, thistles and nettles. Sheep, impervious to the casual human cares of the Saturday ritual, grazed on the outfield and the nominal square for much of the week. The club was still ninety or so years away from the elevated status that took it to the village final at Lord's.

Dip noticed the wanton manner in which many of the local lads in the team slogged and perished on the difficult natural pitches of the day. He was not a boy to be influenced by such reckless bravado; he'd waited for a week for a match and saw no sense then in hastening his departure from the wicket by trying, every ball, to dislodge one of those lofty rooks' nests beyond the boundary. Very consciously, he was already intent on doing things at his own phlegmatic pace.

Farming sons, living in relatively remote parishes in late Victorian and Edwardian times, were apt to accept a way of life which, partly because of geographical limitations, didn't embrace much sense of ambition. Dipper, taciturn by nature, expressed his eloquence through the cheap, yellowing bat in his hands. If ambitions lurked, he kept them to himself.

"Main thing to remember, lad," his father would say, "is that the ball don't get past the bat. Keep them stumps upright." At times the two of them played in the same Apperley side – and so did Mr Gillett, the Mayor of Gloucester. The Mayor had a bristling moustache and smoked a pipe until the moment he walked out to the wicket. There was a nice social cross-section to the team. It showed sartorially, too. Mr Dipper, senior, who was clearly able to rely on other members of his big family to look after the Saturday milking, liked to wear a boater as he fielded. Not all the village players could run to white flannels; one or two kept on their working boots. Historically, however, they played to win. Alf heeded his father and never gave his wicket away.

Nor, it should be added, did the pair of them smile too much. They had a permanent saturnine expression. But that serious countenance should not necessarily imply any lack of friendliness. Look at a hundred sepia prints of early team groups. The poses are stylised, the players appearing self-conscious and inhibited. It was not the fashion to reveal the merest suggestion of relaxation or high spirits. Alf, more the stone-waller than the stroke-maker, a lad who spurned excitement and high drama, was still a popular team-mate. So he should have been. In his own one-paced mode, uncoached though with an eye as sharp as a Severn Vale poacher, he won games for Apperley. Oppositions despaired of getting him out. He may have been a slow scorer – but often he was a victorious one. The hoary stories about his supposed facility for pulling balls into the beds of stinging nettles may have had an element of truth, embroidered in the retelling. What was beyond dispute, even if few of the old scorebooks have survived, was his sheer consistency in compiling runs. Because his timing was so true and he knew the contours of the outfield, he was even then the best batsman in the village side.

Before too long he was playing for Tewkesbury, where the standard was higher and the pitch better prepared. Not that he was privately any happier than he'd been at Apperley. He liked familiar things: the lads of the parish,

156

the sound of the sankeys being rehearsed at the little Methodist building just round the corner from the ground, those bulging rooks' nests, timeless as neighbouring Deerhurst with its Saxon minster and chapel where the Dipper tombstones linger in crumbling and leaning stonework. But the invitation to play for Tewkesbury could hardly be ignored. Encouragement was soon forthcoming, not least from one renowned member of the team, Charlie Parker.

They played side by side for Tewkesbury only a few times. By then, Charlie was on his way to Gloucestershire. He was still bowling at medium-pace and by those pastoral standards already seen as a potential genius. Alf watched him in something approaching awe. Whereas Dip was the silent listener, Charlie with a measure of emergent precocity was holding forth on politics, the derisory wages of an agricultural worker like his father ... and cricket. He always had a ready audience; he broadened the vocabulary of oaths for those who willingly eavesdropped.

Parker reached the county ground in Bristol five years before Dipper. They both played once for their country. Dip felt he was fortunate to be selected. Charlie knew he'd been almost criminally slighted. Only Wilfred Rhodes and Tich Freeman took more wickets. Parker was rebuffed because of his temperament, his undisguised contempt for those in authority. Plum Warner remained his bête noire. The mutual antagonism was virtually tangible. Within the Gloucestershire dressing room, Parker, tetchy and intrepid, was an idol to be cherished. Dipper liked him as a person and admired him as a bowler, just like all his team-mates did.

The two went on to share journeys down to Bristol from the north of the county, and digs on away tours. Charlie continued to do all the talking. In personality, they were extreme opposites. Dip drank halves to Parker's pints. When the Gloucestershire secretary told Dipper his winter salary was being cut to ten shillings a week, Charlie said it was a bloody disgrace. He fought many a battle for his fellow pros; when he wasn't knocking on the committee room door to make a valid if militant point, then he was being summoned there to explain some breech of discipline during the previous match.

Whatever the fiery exchanges, Parker negotiated from strength. He was a great bowler – and an unstinting team man. He and Dipper played their hearts and souls out for the county. Gloucestershire frequently looked a weak side, lacking stability and balance. Spectators lost count of the occasions when Dipper, without backlift or flourish, carried the batting – and Parker the bowling.

The county could never be called flush. Each year there was a painful effort to balance the books. Terms were rarely generous for the players. The officials relied, maybe unreasonably, on old-fashioned qualities like loyalty. Dipper, a man not too troubled by the complexities and wiles of human nature, was loyal. So was Harry Smith, a Bristolian, as adept at keeping wicket as dribbling down the touchline for Bristol Rovers and Bolton Wanderers. So was George Dennett, a sweet-natured left arm spinner who took more than 2000 wickets and yet didn't sniff Test recognition. So – though on principle he would have disputed such a sentimental viewpoint – was Parker.

Dip had made his debut for Gloucestershire in the midsummer of 1908. He was helping on the farm and the summons took him by surprise. The county were due to travel to Tonbridge to play Kent; they couldn't rustle up eleven available and fit players, and Tewkesbury had been advocating Dipper's claims. 'There's nothing stylish about this village feller but no one can get him out.'

Not a bad recommendation, especially for a depleted team. He stuffed his modest, assorted kit into a brown paper bag and caught the train, to meet up with the rest of the county side. He'd never stayed away from home before. Gilbert Jessop, the captain, gave him a friendly welcome but didn't think he looked much like a cricketer: more like, well, a farmer's boy. Jack Board, the wicket keeper, chummily said he used to be a gardener and knew all about growing crops. Dipper, the introvert, nodded; but he didn't feel at home.

The Tonbridge pitch was described by *Wisden* as "treacherous". Dip, who opened for Apperley and Tewkesbury, wondered where he'd be in the order. He wasn't nervous; he wasn't the sort who went in for self-analysis or much contemplation about the strengths of the Kent opposition. "You'll bat at number nine," said Jessop, without explanation to the 22-year-old.

Kent won by an innings. In the second innings Gloucestershire were all out for 62. Of all things, Dip, a batsman who never moved out of his ground and didn't play a shot unless it was necessary, was stumped for eight. That kind of dismissal was rare indeed during a long career. His debut was still not in any sense a failure. From that lowly position in the batting order, he had scored 30 not out, in the first innings. Parker was waiting for him as he came off. "Nothing wrong with that, Alf. Looked as though you'd been playing county cricket for years."

If that was what it was like, Dipper thought, he reckoned he was worth an extended run. Half the team were moaning about the pitch. Hadn't they played on some of those rough-and-ready grounds down country lanes around Deerhurst? He'd remembered what his father had told him each week: "Your job, lad, is to make sure the ball don't knock over the stumps."

He had a dozen matches that season and scored just under 350 runs. Nearer home, at Gloucester Spa, the murmurs of approval were audible around the ground. He was undefeated on 56 in the first innings and reached 64 in the second. The range of the Sussex attack made no obvious impression on him. His future on the farm was coming rapidly to an end. By 1911 – it would surely have been earlier but for the selectors' whims and promises to occasional amateurs over the brandy glasses – Dipper was established in the

county team. He responded by passing 1000 runs. Jessop met Dip's father and, perhaps feeling the need to keep him sweet after the son's recent frustrations, offered him a brace of partridge if the aggregate of runs wasn't bettered in 1912.

It might be thought that Dipper was hardly Jessop's sort of cricketer. While the flamboyant skipper stretched and drove forcefully in a dozen different arcs, the newcomer rejected any semblance of a liberty. He played a dead bat with pride. He turned the ball, with somnolent composure, just wide of mid-wicket for a single when Jessop flashed attractively for four. But Jessop was acutely aware of the dearth of undeviating backbone to the order. Here was a batsman prepared to stay all day. Sometimes he did: without a single stroke to recall or an emotion to manifest. In the following years, however, he would repeatedly sustain hope for Gloucestershire amid wholesale frailties and adventurous follies from transitory players of token pedigree.

In all he carried his bat eleven times for the county. He exasperated opposing bowlers and crowds. Nothing would fluster or agitate him. He was called boring – but never by his own team-mates. Like all the proficient slow coaches, he would occasionally make mischief by unfurling a succession of prodigious blows. He didn't flinch from seemingly histrionic indifference to reputation that few of the more illustrious batsmen of his day dared to demonstrate.

He was a batsman who fancied his bowling. It was slightly less than medium-pace but on a spot. At Gloucester he took 7-87 against Kent. His best was against Leicestershire at Cheltenham the first season after the First World War. A relation or two and friends from the village were in the crowd, dominated by sports-starved local soldiers back from the trenches. Unsmiling, crafty and inwardly exultant, he took 14 wickets from the match.

We come reluctantly to his fielding. It was not his strength. He moved like a stiff-jointed harvest worker rather than an athlete. His gnarled fists held onto the catches that came straight to him but he was deficient of agility and anticipation. In 1921, the same year as Parker, Dipper made his sole Test appearance.

He'd just scored 70 not out for Gloucestershire against the Australians. For the second Test, against the Australians at Lord's, England made six changes. Dipper walked out with D J Knight (two Tests), the schoolmaster-amateur, to open the innings against the ferocity of Gregory and McDonald. Twice he was bowled by McDonald but not before he had scored a defiant and unruffled 40 in the second innings. There was favourable comment on his batting, little alas about his fielding. He was not alone. "The England fielding was well below par, the side being one of the worst fielding combinations ever to represent England in at Test match." Considered judgement could not be more withering than that. There was a large crowd at the country's most famous ground and many spectators squirmed as the runs were given away.

Dip was no more at fault than two or three others amid the general embarrassment. It was still apparently too much to forgive; he was not given another Test.

Nor was he, in fairness, quite the worst fielder in the Gloucestershire side. Too many were inclined to waddle rather than run. The absence of physical alertness and movement became something of a joke. During the mid-Twenties, players were getting old together. They tried to save their legs in the field, relieved when the ball passed them by to reach the boundary. The image of Percy Mills, George Dennett and Dip nominally stationed to cut off the fours is cruelly comical. It was Grahame Parker, player and later manager, who with Charlie Parker's lugubrious assistance, perpetuated the story of the sweltering day when the captain, Douglas Robinson, had an aberration and placed his three poorest fielders to guard the leg side. The ball was struck towards square leg and the seemingly geriatric trio left the retrieving of it to each other. Eventually they realised the ball wasn't going to reach the boundary so cantered off from various directions in gentle pursuit. Parker, the bowler, hands on hips, spluttered: "Just look at that. There go my bloody greyhounds." The batsmen ran five.

Dip must have known his shortcomings. If, after his retirement in 1932 and his brief career as a first class umpire, anyone joked about his fielding, his instant rejoinder would be: "Don't forget I took 210 catches." It's a reasonable statistic, though his career with Gloucestershire was a long one. Like many a solid countryman, he probably didn't like criticism. Not that many criticised him. He was a simple man, strong of shoulder and heart, who gave his county a formidable, if often unglamorous, return. You never heard any of his contemporaries say a snide or unkind word about him.

Hammond, at times as sparing in conversation as the older man, liked him and appreciated the anchor role that Dipper played. Newly arrived in Bristol, not yet influenced by the social aspirations that were to alienate him from some of his colleagues, Hammond was also a listener. He enjoyed the earthy jokes and the gossip, while leaving it to more gregarious pros to do the telling. But he was encouraged more than once, as the tired players gulped their pints of ale at the close, to remind them of the day he scored his first hundred for the county. It was a good and true story.

Dip and Hammond, more or less half his age, opened the innings together against Surrey in 1923. Runs were coming easily enough and for a normally sluggish mover, content usually with singles and twos, Dip was positively frisky. They presented an amusing sight: Wally beautifully built and co-ordinated. Maybe the ageing farmer's son was sensitive about the contrast in athleticism and had a dry-humoured point to make. He started calling for audacious runs and when he caught Hammond mopping his brow between overs, he ambled down the track and asked if the sun was getting to him.

Fielders and team-mates back in the pavilion sensed what was happening. Hammond, slim, boyish and a trifle embarrassed to be seen wiping the sweat from his forehead, eventually caught on. He grinned back. Dipper was out first for 99; his young partner progressed to his century. On the return to the pavilion, Dip was stretched out wearily on the dressing room bench. 'What's the trouble, then – has the sun got to you, Alf?'

The game's historians have probably been remiss in recording so sparingly Dipper's contribution as a county opening batsman. They were no doubt influenced by the ungainly fashion he scored his runs, ignoring in the process the sheer number he accumulated for a side which for a long time, until Hammond arrived, lacked a batsman of dependability. He played 478 matches for Gloucestershire and in all cricket made 28,075 runs at an average of 35.27.

In the nets: Alf Dipper batting, Wally Hammond on the far left

Alfred Ernest Dipper wasn't exactly a character. He had the slightly careworn face of a poker player who tells us nothing about himself or his hand. He had no time for superfluous conversation and had few intellectual pretensions. He liked cricket more than farming. And he liked scoring on the leg side most of all.

I went back to Apperley, where for 250 years there had been Dippers tilling the land. Sadly they have now all gone. All one finds is the treasured old picture in the pavilion and Dipper's Cottage, down the twisting road toward the Coalhouse pub and the banks of the Severn. He was only 60 when he died in 1945, in London. They continue to talk in the village of him with some pride. But the memories, the stories and the deeds are now only recounted at second or third hand. People aren't sure where he is buried. Apperley's Test cricketer, and most famous resident, is no more than a distant name – only vaguely identified by some of the newer parishioners – receding unsentimentally into the past. History can have a remorseless edge.

Maybe it's all to do with the name: Horace Hazell. Could there be anything more evocative, rural-sounding, serene? They used to call him simply "H" or Nutty. His is a name that belongs to Somerset's vibrant hedgerows, fresh, chirpy and wholesome as the morning's dew.

Most of us have a favourite county cricketer, possibly going back to our childhood. He may not be a glamorous sportsman, the archetypal match-winner, fashioned for daily headlines and acclaim. He may even be an ordinary practitioner with bat or ball. We're not always quite sure why we like him best. It's no doubt an amalgam of youthful idolatry on our part, the indefinable appeal of the player's essence and persona, and the subconscious acceptance that he symbolises the spirit of the game we defiantly cherish.

Horace gave up playing for Somerset in 1952 and died in 1990. He remains my favourite, timelessly unrivalled. Yet I never drooled over him or waited in awe for his autograph. There are some aspects of hero worship best left to the second-former; cricket's romantics - an embarrassing breed of which I confess intermittent membership - are, like "anoraks" and heavy rollers, part of the game's furniture. Sometimes they tend to get a little in the way and obscure the true view.

"H" has always been to me that true view. He has been the metaphor for my appreciation of cricket. Jovial, spiritually uplifting, without malice or artifice. Whenever as a boy I went to Taunton, Horace seemed to be bowling (or Harold Gimblett batting). It was slow left-arm, mostly devoid of tricks. Unlike Jack White, who kept him waiting for a place in the county side, Hazell knew nothing of flight. Nor, come to that, did he spin the ball very much. 'Just look at my fingers,' he used to say. 'They're too small to get any spin.'

So what was there left for him? Accuracy, nagging, unwavering accuracy. Farmer White claimed he could land every ball on a sixpence; with his successor, so different in style and build, every delivery pitched on the eye of a needle. Precision was what he dispensed. It sounds soulless and mechanical. So it probably was for the non-partisan. But the nuances were reserved for his team-mates, as he talked incessantly in a voice nurtured on the pastoral, Somerset side of Bristol and which seemed to become more Quantoxhead or Creech St Michael as the years went on. The West Country's stonewallers were rarely bores, as CCC 'Box' Case and Alf Dipper proved. Nor were the slow bowlers who waited for a batsman to lose patience. Once at Taunton in 1949, against Gloucestershire, Hazell sent down 105 balls, more than 17 maidens, without conceding a run. The opposition included at least one renowned stroke-maker in Tom Graveney. 'Just couldn't get him away, don't ask me why,' the England batsman would later reflect.

Horace was rather embarrassed by the record he'd created. 'A good track, and I certainly didn't get many to turn.' He was strong on self-disparagement. 'I felt sorry for the spectators - they'd have liked to see a few more runs from Tom.'

He never quite knew what to make of Gloucestershire. Growing up in Brislington, on the edge of Bristol, he used to walk the four miles from his home to the County Ground to watch his idol, Wally Hammond. One day, he hoped, he'd play for Gloucestershire, but when he went for a trial the county turned him down. That must have been a shattering rejection; he had even worked out a piece of private subterfuge, to use his aunt's address (on the other 'Glos' side of Bristol's Avon) to convince the county secretary that there were no registration problems.

Not that Somerset were noticeably any more enthusiastic. As far as they were concerned, White's only obvious rival for his place was the haymaking field - though he apparently had a compliant father. They had a cursory look at Hazell and then sent him off to London for a second opinion from an indoor school. The report that followed was hardly what anyone expected. 'This little fellow won't make it as a bowler - he's too slow. But if he perseveres, he may have a future as a batsman.'

It was a crazy assessment. The teenager returned to Taunton and talked his way into a contract for ten bob a week. 'Mind you, I wasn't a bad batsman.' True enough, but usually from the number eleven position. We'll return to his acquired batting reputation as The Crisis King.

His county debut came in the Bank Holiday match with Gloucestershire in 1929. He caught the train from Temple Meads, and no-one really knew who this chunky little fellow was. When he'd previously gone to Taunton for a trial, his friends at Brislington CC lent him a bat and a pair of pads. His cricketing wardrobe hadn't been much extended now.

Guy Earle was acting as captain for the first match. 'Tell me, young-em-Hazell, where do you field?'

'Anywhere, sir.' So you did in club cricket.

Earle took no obvious chances; Horace was stationed at mid-on. And in the opening overs, he dropped a sitter. To his surprise, as he'd never fielded there before, he was moved to leg-slip for Arthur Wellard. Immediately he put down another catch. There couldn't have been a worse start, but at least he went on to take a wicket or two.

In the post-war years, when he regularly topped Somerset's bowling averages, Hazell was the most amusingly recognisable figure on the field. He was short and fat. In our reports we discreetly referred to him as rotund. Some of his pals were inclined to call him porky, though it was his lack of inches that accentuated the waistline. He seemed to waddle up to the wicket and, in the late years, the arm was less high. He fielded mostly in the slips, so rigorous chasing of the ball to distant parts was avoided. *Wisden* reminds us that he took some stinging catches off his own bowling. On one of his first visits to the Taunton outdoor nets, the senior pro, Tom Young, handed him the ball and said: 'Now that tall bloke who's just arrived is Mr Earle. Hardest hitter in the club. So as soon as you've let go of the ball, get out of the way!'

Hazell was a mere boy, not perhaps endowed with a surfeit of physical courage. 'The very first ball was belted straight back at me. Couldn't avoid it. Would have gone right through my stomach. I thrust out my hands to protect myself and the ball stuck. Nearly had my thumb off, though.'

For someone not naturally agile, he hung on to most of his catches in the slips. One he didn't, and which went through his legs, was a let-off for

Hammond. Stage-managed coughs all round. Tom Young, who could be critical of the county's young pros, was the bowler who suffered. He made his displeasure very evident.

The drop, and such a crucial one, continued to haunt Horace. 'Back in the dressing room I moved to the basin next to his. I did my best to placate him. I didn't try to let it slip - honest. I think I was forgiven.'

It is probably true to say that over the generations Somerset had more bad fielders than most. Some were embarrassingly bad, driving captains like John Daniell, that handsome lawyer Reggie Ingle, Jack White and Bunty Longrigg to uncontrolled despair at times. Hazell was fine as long as the ball was coming straight to him; once or twice, when batsmen were inelegantly slogging, he was dispatched, with a minimum of confidence, to the outfield. Then the spectators, more in good nature than insensitivity, would chuckle at his misfortunes. Welsh journalists can be less sensitive. There was the afternoon at Cardiff when Ossie Wheatley, without hope or co-ordination, only managed to help the ball on its way over the boundary. The window of the press box was opened and a Celtic literary elder shouted: 'Hey, Ossie, how do you spell awkward?' It didn't go that far with Horace.

Because of his sunny nature and an amiable manner that seldom deserted him, individual lapses were hardly ever held against him. The nearest he came to collective disapproval was in an away game at Chelmsford before the war. 'We had no chance of anything and couldn't wait to get home. As I prepared to go in as last man, I was told there was no need at all to try to score the four runs needed to save the follow-on. In fact, a perfectly good train left Chelmsford at 2.20 p.m.

'Essex, for their part, brought up a silly mid-off, and I intended to pop up the simplest of catches. The trouble was that Ken Farnes was so bloody fast that the ball flew off the edge off my defensive bat for four. And Somerset arrived back in Taunton in the early hours of the morning. Oh dear!'

Hammond remained Hazell's imperishable hero, although his affection for the Gloucestershire team en bloc was limited. He found Somerset altogether more cordial and jokey. Gloucestershire had little to say at the lunch interval. In the middle of the salad, Hazell and Bill Andrews would wink and noisily wish each other 'Good morning' in ironic conviviality. Horace liked a couple of bottles of Bass to help down the limp leaves of lettuce. He once took eight wickets in the immediate post-lunch session - and put it down to energy enhancing from the brewery trade.

On one occasion, Hammond said: 'I'd like that little chap to be playing for me.' We can assume it was after that great left-arm bowler Charlie Parker had gone; he'd have seen it as a sneaky slight. It's possible that Wally was critical of the judgment of those who had decided Hazell, a wholehearted Bristolian, would never be guileful enough for Gloucestershire.

When in 1951 Hammond was persuaded, with an appalling lack of wisdom and dignity on everyone's part, to make a one-off comeback against Somerset at Bristol, Hazell - eternally dotty with admiration - bowled against him. The great batsman scratched around, playing and missing. He had neither timing nor confidence. The Nevil Road ground, full of spectators who had come again to watch and wonder, was eerily silent. We can only begin to contemplate the torment and wretchedness that Wally, florid and overweight, was going through.

'I promise you I was crying. I was actually attempting to give him half-volleys outside the off-stump,' Hazell told me. Those of us who weren't present were the lucky ones. For Horace and all of Wally's other devotees, it was a day of excruciating poignancy.

Somerset, perhaps like no other county, were stacked with characters. They didn't win, or even look like winning, the championship but they were popular visitors to grounds around the country. Someone once said, in the Sixties - even before the triumphant, if contentious, Richards-Botham years - that Somerset were (outside the county itself) everyone's second favourite team. That was a compliment to be treasured. Some of the characters, like half a dozen amateurs we could mention, were never worth their inclusion. Sweat-stained pros like Hazell, Wellard and Andrews were. They were admired as players, loved as persons.

Horace left the playing staff in 1952, meanly offered no more than match terms. Somerset so often lacked good sense and diplomacy when lionhearted players were coming to the end of their meritorious careers. He made 350 appearances and took 957 first-class wickets.

Like most number eleven batsmen he argued that his status was devalued. In truth he offered a cussed straight bat to force unlikely draws a dozen or so times. Despite the roly-poly frame he was boyishly nimble between the wickets. He volunteered to act as runner when team-mates of more illustrious batting pedigrees were limping; maybe it wasn't an accident when one or two actually asked for him.

Home at Brislington and Keynsham, the club from where Marcus Trescothick later emerged, Hazell, the boy batsman, liked to be recognised for his conscientious, defensive batting. But his unpredictability was one of his more endearing traits. At Bath in 1936, he suddenly went after another left-arm spinner of more elevated reputation, Hedley Verity. Four times in an over, Hazell aimed for Great Pulteney Street and hit sixes every bit as high as the church towers that surrounded the ground. 'Careful, H,' shouted Bertie Buse, 'I live just down the road.'

"H" was funny: in the way so few county cricketers are nowadays. He was unsophisticated, countrified (to remind us that Brislington used to be a village remote from Bristol's urban culture) and more chatty than Bill

Andrews. Jokes tumbled out. Poor Wally Luckes, the neatest and most efficient of wicket-keepers, suffered from constipation.

'I've got the answer, Wally - the best laxative of all.'

'And what's that, Nutty?'

'You can get it at Trent Bridge next week. Name of Bill Voce.'

Horace led the sing-songs and his party piece in the dressing room, when Somerset believed they'd benefit from a change of climate, was to strip to the waist and put a towel on his head. Then, in Islamic entreaties, he would cry to Allah for rain. Not quite politically correct by today's social strictures, but his colleagues swore that once at Clacton Hazell's pleas were answered.

He was a team man. When the badly-paid pros slept three to a bed in Bayswater, to save on expenses, the podgy Hazell was allowed a child's couch in the same room. But he readily swapped with Gimblett on one of the occasions. 'Trouble was, Harold was on his way to a hundred, and he was going through every shot in his sleep. That was tough on Arthur and Bill.'

In those sepia days, the pros were on a basic £600 per season, with a small bonus if you scored a hundred or took five wickets. They dutifully paid for their round (though Bertie Buse famously closed his eyes and affected sleep when it was his call). But beer was still cheap and so was the food they picked up from the late-night caffs. Their cricket lunch was their main meal, even if the menu was painfully limited, and Hazell always swore that rabbit was used in the occasional chicken casserole.

Well yes, he did like - and earn - a few drinks. The Somerset boys, again oddly unlike the modern player, would bowl all day and then put away their pints. Those invited to Gimblett's wedding were somewhat disconcerted to discover it was a Non-Conformist affair with the reception in a "dry" hotel. Horace and Bill persuaded the chef to part with a bottle of cooking sherry. This they polished off to reveal the extent of their thirst. After the reception, the two went on a pub crawl to Weston-super-Mare. Hazell was put on the last train back to Bristol; he immediately fell asleep, to be woken at Temple Meads, where he stumbled out and lodged between the edge of the train and the platform. It took four porters to extricate him. As ever, he remained in good humour.

I came to know him best in his late years. By then he was a widower and lonely. He used to wear a little woolly hat and tend the flowers in his back garden, still in Brislington. I'd take along half a bottle of whisky and listen to his stories. I didn't need to prompt him. The eyes would light up again. Once I showed him a photograph of some of his contemporaries, several of whom were by then dead. Spontaneously he put the faded print to his lips and kissed his former team-mates. Nothing could have been more moving.

Somerset in 1939
Horace Hazell, Bertie Buse, Arthur Wellard, Reg Trump (scorer),
Bill Andrews, Frank Lee, Harold Gimblett
Wally Luckes, Dar Lyon, Bunty Longrigg, Jake Seamer, Ken Kinnersley

The memories had never left him, and we can imagine he went to sleep, even into his late 80s, still thinking of those he played with. 'Now there was Johnny Lawrence, a wonderful little leg-spinner. But, oh dear, such a strict Methodist. He used to watch me for ages, then shake his head and say, "You naughty boy, Horace. You smoke and drink far too much." And I suppose I did. RJO (Jack) Meyer wasn't against us having a good time. He also liked to make sure we were all well-fed. Even stopped the Manchester express by pulling the communication cord one night after we'd been playing in London. We'd told him we were hungry - so he asked the anxious guard who turned up what he could do about it. Some sandwiches magically arrived. And RJO wasn't fined, as far as I know, for pulling the chord.'

If the Millfield head was eccentric, what about Sydney Rippon, the father of that important MP, the Right Honourable Geoffrey. 'He once made 99 not out in a new, stiff, uncomfortable pair of pads. In the hotel that night, he walked up and down the bedroom corridor in his pads for two hours. The hotel staff didn't know what was going on. A strange feller, odd in the head. And next morning he was out first ball.' Horace may have taken a liberty with the final fact, but it didn't matter. It's a Hazell special, plucked from Somerset folklore, about an extraordinary amateur who once had to be restrained by Horace and his skipper after being run out by one of the down-the-order professionals.

Somerset cricket was his life: and to me, he was Somerset cricket. He played before and then just after the war when the servicemen had returned, starved of professional sport, to swell the crowds. County cricket still meant something, not yet marginalised by ECB contracts and other pragmatic considerations.

Horace wanted only to play for Gloucestershire or Somerset. He had no other serious ambition. His brother worked on a Bristol newspaper and returned one morning, at 3 a.m., to see the light still on in Horace's bedroom. 'I half-opened the door and found that he'd fallen asleep, with a book of instruction on bowling grips by Fred Root in one hand, a cricket ball in the other. My brother would only have been 13 or 14 at the time.'

Those of us who grew from boys to men, devouring the cricket scores in the daily papers with almost biblical devotion, now glance rather than dally. The game has become more impersonal. There's a transitory aspect to the team sheets. Half the names mean little to us and, in any case, they will be gone by next year. The intimacy and continuity have receded.

I retain images of Horace Hazell, strolling up to the wicket, pretending the ball is turning when it isn't, challenging batsmen to lose their patience and go after him. I see him ambling, tummy bulging and face beaming, from one set of slips to the other. I see him waddling out, the last man and ten to win, with an expression which says, 'Leave it to the Crisis King!' Do you know, someone worked out he was not-out no fewer than 228 times. I see him, a trifle sheepishly, driving off in skipper Stuart Rogers' red sports car. (I asked him years later about that and he said: 'He leaned on me a bit as I was senior professional by this time. He took me off to some swanky restaurant and ordered a couple of bottles of wine. D'you know, wine was the only drink I couldn't manage. Made me drunk as a handcart.') I see him, dark hair sleeked back, walking onto the field with Wellard - half as tall and probably half as fit.

His happiness, in the company of his fellow players, was unconfined. He bubbled with cheeky asides while remaining in awe of those who he inherently knew were better cricketers than he would ever be. Away from the ground, among people who spoke with a more refined accent and joked at his "Bristolese" or gauche expressions, he lacked social confidence. The inferiority complex was never too far away. On the field, there were no airs and graces to trouble him.

'The track's just right for you, Nutty. You'll be on early.'

And he was. As I was saying, he was always on. Wheeling away, looking like a village cricketer. Yet we knew he was much more than that. He was a valued component of a warm-hearted, oddball team. He was a true county cricketer. Patently proud to be an honest pro in the game he loved - a game then which still tingled with humanity.

BIBLIOGRAPHY

Scyld Berry (ed): *The Observer on Cricket* (Unwin Hyman, 1987)

John Billot: *History of Welsh International Rugby* (Roman Way Books, 1999)

Derek Birley: *The Willow Wand* (Simon & Schuster, 1989)

Christopher Brookes: *His Own Man, The Life of Neville Cardus*
(Methuen, 1985)

Alan Gibson: *A Mingled Yarn* (Collins, 1976)

Alan Gibson: *Growing Up With Cricket* (George Allen & Unwin, 1985)

John Harding: *Jack 'Kid' Berg - The Whitechapel Windmill*
(Robson Books, 1987)

Patsy Hendren: *Big Cricket* (Hodder & Stoughton, 1934)

Patsy Hendren: *The Book of Cricket and Cricketers*
(Athletic Publications, 1927)

Jeremy Malies: *Sporting Doubles* (Robson Books, 1998)

Grahame Parker: *Gloucestershire Road* (Pelham Books, 1983)

Alun Richards: *Carwyn, A Personal Memoir* (Michael Joseph, 1984)

R.C. Robertson-Glasgow: *Cricket Prints* (Sportsman's Book Club, 1943)

R.C. Robertson-Glasgow: *46 Not Out* (Hollis & Carter, 1948)

R.C. Robertson-Glasgow: *All In The Game* (Dennis Dobson, 1952)

R.C. Robertson-Glasgow: *Country Talk* (The Country Book Club, 1966)

Alan Ross (ed): *Crusoe on Cricket* (Pavilion Books, 1985)

Alec Stock, Bryon Butler (ed): *Football Club Manager*
(Sportsman's Book Club, 1969)

Chris Westcott: *Class of '59* (Mainstream Publishing, 2000)

Wisden Cricketers' Almanack.

The Times, The Guardian, Western Mail and *Men Only.*

INDEX